A Compendious

HISTORY

OF THE

Old *and* New Teſtament,

Extracted from the

HOLY BIBLE.

AND

Adapted to all Capacities.

Whereby, the *Reader* may be enabled, in an *Eaſy, Pleaſant*, and *Speedy Manner*, to become *Learned* in the SACRED SCRIPTURES.

Interſperſed with ſuitable Reflections.

And Adorned with 120 Curious COPPER CUTS, lively repreſenting each HISTORY.

The SECOND EDITION, *Corrected.*

LONDON:
Printed for J. HAZARD, at the *Bible*, near *Stationers-Hall.* M.DCC.XXXIV.

Wipf and Stock Publishers • Eugene, Oregon

Edited and composed by A K M Adam

Typeset in
I M Fell DW Pica Pro

The Fell Types are digitally reproduced by Igino Marini.
www.iginomarini.com

Second edition of *A Compendious History of the Old and New Teſtament, Extracted from the holy Bible and Adapted to all Capacities* originally published, London : J. Hazard, 1734.

Paperback: 978-1-5326-1636-5

Hardcover: 978-1-4982-4010-9

Wipf & Stock
An imprint of Wipf and Stock Publiſhers
199 Weſt 8th Avenue
Eugene, OR 97401

www.wipfandstock.com

Manufactured in the U.S.A.

THE PREFACE.

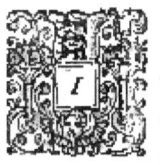 *T is altogether unnecessary to trouble the Reader with a Detail of the Usefulness of the following Sheets; since every Thing that bears so intimate a Relation to the Holy Bible, carries with it its own Recommendation.*

The Expence of purchasing the Sieur de Royamont's *History of the Bible, publish'd by Mr.* Blome; *and of that more excellent one written by Mr.* Howell, *was a great Inducement to us, to offer this small Piece to the World: — Most of the Historical Facts (in the Old Testament especially) want no Explanation or Comment, and it must, in some Measure, render the Design of those Pieces less valuable, as the Sacred Books themselves, of almost any Size, may be purchased at a much easier Rate, than the Comments on them: For who would not rather have Recourse to the Fountain-*

Head of Knowledge, than to the Under-Currents? Especially when it is impossible that most of the Facts can be set in a clearer or fuller Light, than they already shine in, as related with the beautiful Simplicity so natural to the inspired Penmen, who have transmitted to us the Sacred History.

'Tis true, the many Copper Plates inserted in those Works, in order to allure the Minds of the Readers to the Study of the Holy Scriptures, necessarily inhance their Price: But if they are generally the Minds of weak Persons, of People of low Education, and of Children, that Pictures are intended to allure, the great Bulk and high Price of those Performances, must consequence, as we have hinted, be a Hindrance to their very Design.

For these Reasons, we thought we should hit upon a proper Medium, and answer all the Ends that are necessary to recommend such a Performance, if we could comprize a History of the Holy Bible in so small a Compass, as to make it proper for Schools, and to allure, by neat Plates, representing many of the most material Facts, the Minds of Youth to the Knowledge of the Scriptures, and which should be afforded at so easy a Price, as that the Expence should be no greater a Burthen to the Parents Pockets, than the Matter of it should be to the Learner's Memory: And which, at the same Time that it should want nothing to make it perfectly intelligible to the meanest Understanding, should not be so low as to merit the Contempt of those of brighter Intellects.

How well we have executed this Design, must be left to the Reader's Determination: But we flatter our selves that we shall stand in some measure acquitted, when he is inform'd of the Difficulty we have labour'd under, from the narrow Compass to which we have been confined, to observe any tolerable Connexion in the respective Histories; especially as the Choice of the several Stories were left to the Designer, who had finished all the Plates before we began to compile; which laid us under an Obligation to write to the Cuts; and frequently to omit some Histories that otherwise ought to have been inserted, for the better Illustration of the Design: As to the rest, it must be confess'd, the Engraver has perform'd his Part, considering his narrow Compass, with an Exquisiteness and Accuracy not to be equalled in several Pieces, where the Artist has had far more Advantages and Room to inable him to excel. But 'tis an ungenerous Part to recommend our selves on the Faults and Imperfections of others; and therefore we shall say no more on this Head.

 We have intersperfed as often as we could, brief Observations and Reflections upon the Histories recited, in order to lead ductile Minds into a Way of Thinking suitable to the Design of each particular Relation: But the Brevity which we were obliged to observe, has laid us under a Necessity of being more sparing on this Head, than we should otherwise have been. And that we might do Justice to the Sacred Text, we have, as often as we could, confident with our intended

Concifeness, chosen to express our selves in the very Words of Scripture.

   As to the rest, we shall only add, *That* if any little Incongruity has been occasion'd by the Choice of the Plates, as in particular in the Passion of our Blessed Lord, his Resurrection, Ascension, &c. which, as they have been taken from the several Relations given thereof by the several Evangelists, may seem to some Readers to favour of Tautology or Repetition ; we have excus'd our selves on that Head by brief Prefaces and References in their proper Places, and shall say no more of them here: But conclude with submitting the whole Performance to the favourable Censure of the Candid Reader.

Gen: 2. 3. 4. cap:
Adam and Eve

droue out of Eden

8 And y^e Lord god planted a garden, &c:
16 And y^e Lord god comanded y^e man, &c
25 And they were both naked, &c:
III 24 So he droue out y^e man, & he placed

I.
The CREATION.

GOD having, out of a confused and obscure *Chaos*, created the Heavens, the Earth, and the Sea; the Fishes, the Birds of the Air, the Cattle, and every creeping Thing, He last of all, was pleased to form *Man*, to be the Lord of all these, *out of the Dust of the Earth*, and *breathed into his Nostrils the Breath of Life*. And that he might not be without a Companion, or *Help meet for him*, he cast the Man into a deep Sleep, and from one of his Ribs, formed Woman, and brought her to the Man, who received her as *Bone of his Bone*, and *Flesh of his Flesh*, and called her *Woman*, to signify her Relation to him.

II.
The FALL.

THIS happy Pair, thus created and placed in Paradise, of all the Works of His Creation, God prohibited them no Enjoyment, saving, that they should not, on Pain of Death, eat of the Fruit of one Tree, called *The Tree of the Knowledge of Good and Evil*; which Command was inforced upon them, as a Test of their Obedience and Acknowledgment of their Dependance upon their Creator. But long had they not enjoy'd the charming Beauties of their Situation, before the Woman, tempted by the wily Serpent, prevailed on the Man to eat of the forbidden Fruit. This their Transgression, could not be hidden from the Eye of an all-seeing God, who upbraiding the Man for his Disobedience, pronounced Sentence upon him, *That, as he was taken out of the Dust, so he should return to Dust again*, and expelled them both out of Paradise.

III.

The Sacrifice of CAIN and ABEL.

FROM this Difobedience of our firft Parents, Rancour, Malice, Revenge, and all the deadly Paffions, began to invade the Heart of Man; and Satan, who had but too well fucceeded in his firft Attempts, never ceafed to purfue the Advantages he had gained: A fatal Example of which happen'd in the Cafe of *Cain* and *Abel*, the Sons of *Adam* and *Eve*: *Cain* being an Husbandman, offered to God, a Sacrifice of fome of his Fruits, and *Abel*, who was a Shepherd, the beft of his Flocks, *Cain*, burning with Refentment and Uncharitablenefs to his Brother, found his Sacrifice unpleafing to God; while that of *Abel* was well accepted, by Reafon of the Integrity of his Heart. This fo irritated *Cain*, that he determined from that Time to wreak his Revenge on his innocent Brother.

IV.

CAIN *flayeth* ABEL.

IN Order to this, *Cain* having treacheroufly inticed *Abel* into the Fields, who little fufpected his barbarous Intention, he there, laying afide all Humanity and Brotherly Affection, rofe up againft him, and flew him. But the Blood of righteous *Abel* crying out from the Earth unto the Lord, the Almighty fet a Mark upon *Cain*, that no Body fhould flay him, but that he might live to bear the tormenting Stings of a wounded Confcience, and condemned him to be a Vagabond upon the Earth all his Life: A juft Punifhment for fuch a barbarous Fratricide, and a Warning to all Pofterity, to avoid the favage Paffions of Envy and Revenge, and all Uncharitablenefs.

Cain & Abels sacrifice

Cain slayeth Abel

III.3 Cain brought of y^e frute of y^e ground
4 And Abell he also brought of y^e fatling
of his flock, and the fat thereof &c:
8 Cain rose up against Abel his brother &

Noah entreth the Ark. Gen: 7:1.

The waters prevail. 7:12.

Gen: 7:1. And y^e Lord said unto Noah, come thou and all thy house into it
Gen: 7:12 And y^e rain was upon y^e earth fortie dayes and fortie nights &c:

V.

The ARK.

THE Sins of Mankind still increasing, and every Generation growing worse and worse, insomuch that there was but one righteous Man to be found; the Almighty, justly provoked at their Ingratitude and Degeneracy, repented him that he had made Man, and resolved to extirpate him from the Face of the Earth: But because the righteous *Noah* should not lose his Reward, God commanded him to build an Ark, according to the Proportions he prescribed, in order to save his own Family, and the living Creatures God should send him. This Ark was a Hundred Years in building, during all which Time, *Noah* preached Repentance to the Sons of Men, in order to avert the Wrath of Heaven; but all to no Purpose, their Hearts being harden'd, and they being abandon'd to their own Destruction.

VI.

The DELUGE.

ALL *Noah's* Admonitions thus proving ineffectual, God commanded him to enter the Ark, which he had stor'd with all necessary Provisions for himself and the Creatures he took with him (every clean Beast by Seven's, and unclean by Two's) together with his Wife, and his Three Sons and their Wives: Which being done, the Lord caused such violent Rains to be shower'd down, for the Space of Forty Days and Forty Nights, that the Earth was totally overwhelm'd, and the Waters prevailed Fifteen Cubits above the highest Hills and Mountains; so that in this universal Deluge, not only Men, but Birds, and Beasts, and every creeping Thing perish'd; except *Noah* and his Family, and the living Creatures with him in the *Ark*; which by the Providence of God was still preserv'd floating on the Surface of the Waters.

VII.

The Waters *dried up*

IT was for the Space of Seven Months from the Beginning of the Flood, that the Earth remain'd overwhelm'd, when the Lord caufed a great Wind to pafs over it, which abated the Waters fo much, that the Ark refted upon the Mountains of *Ararat.* Four Months after which, *Noah* fent forth firft a Raven, which did not return, and after that a Dove, which finding no Refting place, returned to him ; but Seven Days after that, he fent forth the fame Dove, which returned to him with a green Olive-branch in its Mouth, pluck'd off of a Tree; by which *Noah* obferv'd that the Waters were abated. Afterwards, they being wholly dried up, the Lord permitted *Noah*, who had continued in the Ark for a whole Year, to depart from it, together with all his Family, and the living Creatures of all Kinds, that had been preferved therein.

VIII.

GOD's *Covenant with* NOAH.

NOAH, to fhew his Thankfulnefs to the Lord, for his diftinguifhing Mercy and Goodnefs to him, as foon as he came forth of the Ark, built an Altar, and offer'd upon it an Offering of every clean Beaft and every clean Fowl ; which the Almighty was pleafed to accept gracioufly, and made an eternal Covenant with him and his Children, and eftablifh'd as a Token thereof, the Rainbow, to fignify that he would never more deftroy the World by a Deluge, and commanded them to increafe and multiply, and to replenifh and poffefs the Earth.

The waters dried up. 8:16.

Gods Covenāt wth Noah Gen: 9. 13.

Gen: 8.16. Go forth of ye Ark, thou and thy wife, & thy sons, & thy sons wiues &c
Gen: 9.13. I do set my bow in ye cloud, & it shall be for a token of ye Covenant &c

Abra: entertaineth y Angels Gen: 18 8
9

Lot and his two Daugters Gen: 19:32
10

Gen: 18.8 And he took butter & milk
and y.e calfe which he had dressed &c:
Gen:19:32 Come let us make our fa:r
drink wine and we will lie w:th him

IX.
ABRAHAM *entertaineth three* Angels.

MANY Hundred Years after the Death of Noah, it pleafed God to diftinguifh by his Mercies, the faithful *Abraham*, the Son of *Terah*, and Defcendant of *Shem*, one of the Sons of *Noah*; whom he promifed to make the Father and Head of many powerful Nations: And when *Abraham* was a Hundred Years old, he fent Three Angels to his Abode to confirm his Promife; who being received as Travellers by *Abraham*, declared that his Wife would fhortly conceive a Son, which fhe over-hearing, being above Ninety Years of Age, and always barren, laughed at as an impoffible Thing. The Angels challenging her with her Incredulity, fhe, filled with Confufion, not thinking they had heard her, denied fhe had laughed; upon which they reprimanded her, and took leave of *Abraham*, and departed.

X. LOT's *Inceft*.

BUT whilft *Abraham* became the chofen Favourite of the Almighty, it happened not fo well with his Nephew *Lot*, who having feparated from him, by means of the little Brangles and Strifes arifen between their Servants, took up his Abode near the City of *Sodom*, which, for its abominable Wickednefs, being fhortly after deftroyed by Fire and Brimftone from Heaven, and his Wife, for her Difobedience, turned into a Pillar of Salt, and he being driven for Refuge to a Cave in *Zoar*, his Two Daughters, thinking all Mankind but themfelves and their Father, were deftroyed, in order to preferve the Human Species, made him drunk with Wine, and caufed him to commit Inceft; from which unnatural Sin fprang the Fathers of the *Moabites* and the *Ammonites*, Two very powerful Nations.

XI.

HAGAR's *Distress*

BUT before the set Time of the Lord's Promise of a Son to *Abraham*, was accomplished, Sarah recommended to him her Handmaid *Hagar*, as was frequently the Custom of those Days, that he might not be destitute of an Heir, in Case she herself should bear him no Children: Accordingly, *Abraham* had a Son by *Hagar*, called *Ishmael*, who when *Isaac* was born, deriding him, and Hagar behaving herself also unseemly to her Mistress, *Abraham* was obliged to put her and her Son away; who travelling in the Wilderness of *Beersheba*, and being in great Distress for Water, she cast the Child under one of the Shrubs, and removing a Bow-shot Distance, bewail'd her unhappy Case, and her Infant's, whose Death she instantly expected: But the Angel of the Lord discover'd to her a Well of Water, wherewith she saved her Child's Life, who afterwards became the Father of a mighty People called the *Ishmaelites*.

XII.

ABRAHAM's *Tryal*

THE *Jewish* Tradition tells us, that *Isaac* was Thirty-seven Years old when his Father *Abraham* was called upon to the greatest Tryal of his Faith, which he had ever experienc'd. He was not only the Son of the Promise, and the Son of his Parents old Age, but their only earthly Delight and Pleasure: Yet so great was the Faith of *Abraham*, and his Reliance on the Almighty, that when God commanded him, to take this his only Comfort, and sacrifice him to him, he readily, without Hesitation, complied with the divine Command; and as he was just about to slay his Son, the Angel of the Lord called to him to desist, and having applauded his great Faith, caused a Ram to be caught by the Horns in a Thicket, which *Abraham* took and offer'd up to the Lord instead of his Son.

The HISTORY of the BIBLE 13

Hagars Distress Gen XXI: 7

Abrams triall Gen: 22: 10:

16: 7 And y^e Angel of the Lord
found her by a fountain &c:
22: 10 And Abraham stretched forth
his hand and tooke his knife &c:

Isaac and Rebekah Gen: 24:17

Abraham's burial Gen: 25:9

Gen: 24:17 And ye servant ran to meet her & said Let me (I pray thee) drink &c.
Gen: 25:9. And his sons Isaac and Ismael buried him in ye cave of Machpelalah

XIII.

ISAAC and REBEKAH

ABRAHAM having buried his Wife *Sarah*, at the Age of 127 Years, and being old himſelf, thought it Time to Think of marrying his Son *Iſaac*, but not caring to wed him to the Daughters of the Land, he ſent his faithful Steward *Eliezer*, with Camels and a great Equipage, to get him a Wife among the Daughters of his Brother *Nahor* the *Meſopotamian* : The Steward arriving near the City of *Nahor*, by a Well's Side, pray'd to the Lord, That the Damſel, who ſhould be the Wife of *Iſaac*, might come forth with a Pitcher to draw Water, and that if he asked her to give him to drink, me would offer to make his Camels drink alſo : This happen'd according to his Prayer, and Rebekah the Daughter of *Bethuel*, *Nahor*'s Son, coming forth, and offering him and his Camels Drink, he plainly perceived the Finger of the Lord in the Caſe, and inſtantly went home with her, and demanded and obtained her for a Wife for his young Maſter *Iſaac*, and conducted her to him accordingly.

XIV.

ABRAHAM's *Burial.*

AFTER *Abraham* had ſeen his Son *Iſaac* thus happily married, he took to himſelf another Wife, named *Keturah* ; who bore to him Six Sons ; and having preſented theſe Sons with Gifts, he ſent them away towards the *Eaſt Country*, and left all the Remainder of his great Riches to his beloved Son *Iſaac*. And now, having compleated an Hundred and Threeſcore and Fifteen Years, he gave up the Ghoſt, and was buried by his Sons *Iſaac* and *Iſhmael*, in the Cave of *Machſelah*, which he had purchaſed in his Life Time for the Sepulture of his Family, and where he had before buried *Sarah* his Wife.

XV.

ESAU *sells his Birth-Right.*

ISAAC had been marry'd to his beloved Wife *Rebekah* 20 Years, before he had any Children by her and then she conceived of Twins, the first-born whereof was called *Esau*, and the other *Jacob* : When these Sons were grown up, *Esau* became a great Hunter, and *Jacob was a plain Man dwelling in Tents*. It happened that Esau on a Time returning from Hunting ready to faint with Hunger, besought *Jacob*, who had sod Lentile-pottage, to give him a Mess to eat, but *Jacob*, taking Advantage of his Brother's Necessity, insisted upon his parting with his Birth-Right for it. *And* Esau *said, Behold I am at the Point to die ; and what Profit shall this Birth-Right do to me? And* Jacob *said, Swear to me this Day, and he swore unto him : And he sold his Birth-Right unto* Jacob. — Thus Esau *despised his Birth-Right.*

XVI.

JACOB *steals the Blessing from* ESAU.

NOW Isaac *loved* Esau, *because he eat of his Venison* ; *but* Rebekah *loved* Isaac : And hearing *Isaac*, who was now blind with Age, give order to *Esau* to kill him some Venison, and to make savoury Meat for him, that he might bless him before he dy'd, she contriv'd to put *Jacob* in his Stead, and to make him steal from *Esau* the Blessing design'd him ; and accordingly having made *Esau* believe the Imposture, he blessed him, and assured him, that all his Brethren should serve him. *Esau* returning, and *Isaac* being undeceived, would not however reverse his Blessing, but told him, that he should serve his Younger Brother. At which *Esau*, conceived a violent Hatred against *Jacob*, and threatned to kill him after the Death of his Father *Isaac*.

The HISTORY *of the* BIBLE   17

Iacob and Esau Gen: 25:31

Rebekah and Iacob Gen: 27: 8.

Gen: 25:31 And Iacob said sell mee this day thy birth right. And Esau said &c
Gen: 27:8 Now therefore my son obey my voyce, according to that wᶜʰ I &c:

Iacob's Ladder Gen. 28:12

Iacob and Rachel Gen: 29: 3

Gen: 28:12 And he dreamed and behold
a ladder set upon yͤ earth & yͤ top o͡t
Gen: 29:3 And they rolled yͤ stone fro
yͤ wells mouth & watred yͤ sheep &c

XVII.
JACOB's *Ladder*.

JACOB being obliged to flee to avoid the Resentment of his Brother *Esau*, bent his Course to his Mother's Kindred in *Mesopotamia* ; but being belated in his Journey, he gathered some Stones together for his Pillow, and laying him down, fell asleep, and *dream'd, and behold a Ladder set upon the Earth, and the Top of it reach'd to Heaven ; and the Angels of God ascending and descending on it* ; and above it stood the Almighty, who was graciously pleased to renew to him, all the Promises which he had made to *Abraham*, and to *Isaac*, and that he would protect him and bless him in all his Undertakings. *And* Jacob *awaked out of his Sleep, and said, Surely the Lord is in this Place, and I knew it not.* And he vow'd a Vow, that the Lord should be his God, if he would vouchsafe to protect him, and (being not solicitous for ought but the Necessities of Life) if he would be pleas'd to give him Meat to eat, and Raiment to put on ; and he called the Name of the Place *Beth-el*.

XVIII.
JACOB *and* RACHEL.

JACOB pursuing his Journey, arriv'd at a Well in *Haran*, where they used to water their Flocks, and being informed that *Rachel* the Daughter of *Laban* his Mother's Brother, was approaching with her Flock, he rolled a great Stone from the Mouth of the Well, and making himself known to *Rachel*, water'd her Flock ; and she hasten'd to acquaint her Father with his Arrival, who received him with all manner of Kindness ; and he serv'd him 14 Years for his Daughters *Leah* and *Rachel*, and in the Space of 6 Years more, having greatly increased his Substance, and by his Wives and their Handmaids, having 11 Sons, and one Daughter, he set out to return to his Father's House, hoping by this Time his Brother *Esau* had forgot his Resentment.

XIX.

JACOB *wrestles with an* Angel.

JACOB hearing his Brother *Esau* was coming to meet him, attended with 400 Men, was exceeding terrified, and having implored the Divine Protection, he pick'd out 200 *She-Goats, and* 20 *He-Goats* : 200 *Ews, and* 20 *Rams* ; 30 *Milch Camels with their Colts* ; 40 *Kine, and* 10 *Bulls* ; 20 *She-Asses, and* 10 *Foles*, ordering them to be drove before in different Flocks, as Presents to pacify the Fury of his Brother. And he following after alone, was wrestled with by a Man, who proved to be an Angel of the Lord, who touching the Hallow of *Jacob*'s Thigh, occasioned him to halt ever after ; and for this Reason *the Children of* Israel *eat not of the Sinew which shrank, which is upon the Hollow of the Thigh, unto this Day.*

XX.

JACOB *meeteth* ESAU.

JACOB being convinced that the Person he had wrestled with, was an Angel of the Lord, who chang'd his Name to *Israel*, procur'd his Blessing, and departed to meet *Esau* ; who by this Time having approached his People, and being softned by his Brother's humble Deportment laid aside his Resentments, and meeting him, fell on his Neck and kissed him, and wept. *Jacob* presented to him his Wives, and his Sons, and Daughter, and urged him to accept of the Presents he had selected from his Flocks for him ; which, after some Difficulty, *Esau* complying with, many mutual Civilities passed between them, and they parted. And thus was *Jacob* reconciled to his Brother, and delivered from all his Apprehensions on that Score, by his submissive and obliging Deportment to his Brother.

The HISTORY of the BIBLE   21

Iacob and ỹ Angel Gen 32:24

Iacob meeteth Esau Gen: 33:24

Gen:32:24: And there wresled a man
with him untill ỹ breaking of ỹ day.
Gen:33:4 And Esau ran to meet him
and embraced him and fett on &c:

Dinah Ravished Gen: 34 : 2.

The Shechemites slain 34 26

And when Shechem y͞e Son of Hamor
or y͞e Hevite Prince of y͞e countrey &c:
And they slew Hamor and Shechem
his son with y͞e edge of the sword &c.

XXI.
DINAH *Ravished*.

JACOB having thus escaped the Fury of his Brother, pursued his Journey to *Succoth*, and purchased a Field wherein he pitch'd his Tents, and built him an House, and erected an Altar to the Lord. But long he had not been settled there, before *Dinah* his Daughter, out of womanish Curiosity, going to see the Daughters, of the Land, *Shechem* the Son of *Hamor*, Prince of the Country, seized on her by Force, and ravish'd her : But being captivated with her Beauty, he procur'd his Father *Hamor* to treat with *Jacob* about marrying her ; offering to agree to any Proposals that should be made for that purpose, and to consolidate an intire Union between their Families and People, in order to repair the Fault committed by his Son.

XXII.
The Shechemites *slain.*

TO these Proposals *Jacob* and his Son seemed to give Ear, and demanded that the Prince and all the Males of the Country should be Circumcised : To which they readily yielding, on the Third Day, when their Pains were most violent, *Simeon* and *Levi*, Two of the Sons of *Jacob*, unknown to their Father, boldly enter'd the City, and put to the Sword all the Males, not sparing either *Hamor* the King, or his Son *Shechem*, while the whole City became the Plunder of the other Sons, and the Wives and Daughters of the *Shechemites*, were carry'd by them into Captivity. This Bloody Execution sorely vexed *Jacob*, who expostulated with them thereupon in strong Terms ; but they justified themselves because of the Outrage their Sister *Dinah* had received : And the Lord cast a Terror upon all the Nations round about, so that they durst not rise and revenge upon

Jacob, who was innocent of his Sons Violence, the Deſtruction of the *Shechemites*.

XXIII.
JUDAH *and* TAMAR.

JUDAH, one of the Sons of *Jacob*, having Three Sons, Two of which for their Wickedneſs were ſlain by the Lord, he ordered *Tamar* their Widow to dwell with him till his Third Son was grown up, whom he promis'd to give to her in Marriage. But his Son being arriv'd at Maturity, and *Judah* neglecting his Promiſe, *Tamar* chang'd her Apparel for that of a looſe Woman, and went and ſat herſelf down by the Highway-ſide, where *Judah* was to come by : Who taking her for what ſhe appear'd to be, left his Bracelet, Signet, and Staff with her, as Pledges for a Preſent of a Kid which he was to ſend her for her Permiſſion to lie with her ; and ſo, unknown to himſelf, went to Bed to his Daughter-in-Law. Which furniſhes a Leſſon to all Perſons who ſuffer themſelves to be led by their headſtrong Paſſions, that they know not to what Sins their Follies may lead them.

XXIV.
TAMAR *to be burnt.*

JUDAH, as ſoon as he got to his Flock, ſent the Kid to redeem his Pledges, by the Hands of a Friend ; but finding no Woman there, he durſt not, for fear of Scandal, make farther Enquiry. But afterwards hearing that *Tamar* was with Child, he order'd her to be burnt : When ſhe was brought forth, ſhe ſent her Pledges to *Judah*, ſaying, *By the Man whoſe theſe are, am I with Child. And* Judah *acknowledged them, and ſaid, She is more righteous than I, becauſe that I gave her not to* Shelah *my Son: And he knew her no more. Tamar* being thus reſpited from Execution, was in Proceſs of Time deliver'd of Twins.

The HISTORY of the BIBLE

Iudah's incest Gen: 38 : 18

23

Tamar to be burnt: 38 : 24

24

And he said what pledge shall I giue
and she said thy Signet and &c:
And Iudah said bring her forth and
let her be burnt &c.

Joseph's dreams. 37.: 7

Joseph cast into a Pit Gen. 37. 24.

Gen: 37. 7. For behold we were binding sheaves in the field and to my &c:
Gen: 37: 27. Come let us sell him to ye Ishmelites and lett not our hands &c

XXV.
JOSEPH's *Dreams*.

IT frequently happens, that Parents who have several Children, are too apt to shew a partial Affection to some one, tho by this Imprudence they subject their Favourite to the Hatred and Malice of all the rest. This was the Case with *Jacob*, who of all his Sons, loved *Joseph* the Son of *Rachel* best, and was so impolitick as to distinguish him in his Apparel, by cloathing him in gay and party-colour'd Vestments which irritated his Brethren against him. *Joseph*, as is the Case often of the most favour'd, also added to their Disgusts, by acquainting his Father with their Faults and undue Liberties of Speech; and what still augmented their Hatred, was, Two Dreams which he had, and told them of; the one, that as they were binding Sheaves, his Sheaf arose, and stood in the midst of theirs, and that theirs made Obeisance to his Sheaf; the other, that the Sun, Moon and Eleven Stars, paid also Obeisance to him; both which seem'd to presage his future Grandeur and Elevation.

XXVI. JOSEPH *cast into a Pit.*

ALL these Provocations put together, so exasperated *Joseph*'s Brethren against him, that they resolved to wreak their Revenge upon him the first Opportunity. Accordingly *Jacob* having sent him to see how his Brethren fared, who kept their Flocks in a distant Part of the Country, they no sooner saw him, but they conspired together to slay the *Dreamer*, as they called him in Derision. But *Reuben*, his eldest Brother, dissuaded them from their bloody Purpose, and advised them to put him into an empty Pit in the Wilderness, and leave him to his Fate, designing afterwards secretly to deliver him from thence. Accordingly they seized *Joseph*, and having, with great Contumely, stripped him of his party-colour'd Coat, they cast him into a Pit, and sat themselves down to eat and be merry.

XXVII. JOSEPH *fold to the* Ishmaelites.

JOSEPH had not been long in the Pit, when his Brethren saw some *Midianitish* Merchants passing by, to whom they thought they had better sell him, than to be guilty of his Blood : Accordingly they bargained for 20 Pieces of Silver, and delivered him to the *Ishmaelites*, who being on a Journey to Egypt, carried *Joseph* thither, and sold him to *Potiphar*, Captain of the Guards to King *Pharoah*. Mean time *Reuben*, who had a Design privately to save *Joseph*, and knew nothing of his being sold, coming to the Pit, and finding him not there, gave way to the most excessive Grief, and went to his Brethren, telling them, That he found *Joseph* was no more ; and that they should never be able to see their Father's Face: Hereupon they killed a Kid, and dipping *Joseph*'s Coat in the Blood, they carried it to *Jacob*, pretending that some evil Beast had devoured his beloved Son ; which he believing, rent his Cloaths, and cloathed his Loins with Sackcloth, and would not receive any Consolation.

XXVIII. JOSEPH's *Chastity*.

BUT what *Joseph*'s Brethren had designed for his Ruin, by the Providence of God, was turned to his Exaltation ; for *Potiphar* his Master observing his Diligence, and that every thing prospered that he took in Hand, made him Steward over all his Houshold and Estate. In this advantageous Situation he had not continued long, before his Mistress observing him to be a very handsome Youth, tempted him to lie with her : But he abhorring such Wickedness, did all he could to avoid her Company and Conversation ; but on a Time, the Duties of his Office obliging him to be in the House all alone with his Mistress, and no Body being near, she caught hold of his Garment, saying, *Lie with me*. *Joseph* hereupon struggling to get free, left his Garment in her Hand, and fled from the House, to avoid her farther Importunities.

Ioseph sold for 20 pieces. Gen: 37:28

Ioseph resisteth his mistress 39:12

Gen: 37: 28. Then there passed by Midi
anites marchant men &c:
Gen: 39:12 And she caught him by
his gament saying lie with mee &c

Rahab's covenant Iosh: 2:12

12 stones taken out of Jordan Iosh: 4:2

Iosh: 2:12 Now therefore I pray you swear
unto me by yᵉ Lord since I haue &c:
Iosh: 4:2. Take you 12 men out of the
people out of every tribe, a man &c

XXIX. RAHAB's *Covenant*.

AS it is impossible in this small Volume to carry on a strict Connexion in all the Histories of the *Holy Bible*, we shall refer our Readers to the 39th, 40th, and following Chapters of the Book of *Genesis*, for the farther Particulars of the History of *Joseph*; where he will find, how he was imprisoned by the false Accusation of his Mistress: By what Means he was delivered and made *Pharaoh*'s Prime Minister: How he amused his Brethren, who, according to his Dreams, were obliged to submit to him. How he made himself known to them; and of his Grandeur, Riches, Children, Death and Burial. In the Beginning of *Exodus* will be found, the Oppression of the Children of *Israel* in *Egypt* under a new King, their Deliverance by the Hand of *Moses*, &c. who dying, *Joshua*, after many Dangers and great Atchievements, conducted the *Israelites* to the Land of *Promise*; and sending two Spies to the chief City *Jericho*, to view it, they took up their Lodging at the House of a Harlot named *Rahab*, who, covenanting that they should save her and her Family when they took the Town, hid them from the Citizens, who suspected their Errand, and letting them out of her Window by a Cord, they, pursuing her Advice, got off safe.

XXX. STONES *taken out of* Jordan.

THE Spies having encouraged the People to attack *Jericho*, *Joshua* made Preparations accordingly; but being to pass the River *Jordan*, God commanded the Priests to carry the Ark of the Covenant into *Jordan*, the Waters of which he caused to divide as soon as their Feet touched the Brim thereof, and they were gathered up on Heaps, while the Priests enter'd into the midst of the River with the Ark, and there stood, till all the People were passed over; when the Waters returned into their natural Channel, and flowed as before. To perpetuate the Memory of which Prodigy, God commanded that 12 Men out of the 12 Tribes should each take a Stone out of *Jordan*, while the Stream was stopped which *Joshua* pitch'd in *Gilgal*.

XXXI.

CIRCUMCISION *renewed*.

THE Children of *Ifrael* who came out of *Egypt*, having, in their Journey to the Land of *Promife*, behaved themfelves difobediently to the Lord, and often murmur'd againft the Divine Commands; it pleafed God to punifh them, by caufing them to walk forty Years in the *Wildernefs*, during which Time, all that Generation was confumed : And their Defcendants having never been Circumcifed, by Reafon of their being born in their Journeyings, the Lord commanded *Jofhua*, after he had paffed *Jordan*, to caufe all the Males to be initiated into that holy Ordinance, which was accordingly performed, *and they abode in their Places in the Camp till they were whole.*

XXXII.

JERICHO *taken*.

THE Lord being willing to manifeft his Wonders to the Children of *Ifrael*, and to fhew them that they fhould not truft in the Arm of Flefh for their Victories, ordered that the Ark of the Covenant fhould be carried Seven Times round *Jericho*, preceded by Seven Priefts, blowing each a trumpet of Ramfhorns; and at the feventh Time, upon a particular Signal, the People were ordered to give a great Shout, and immediately the lofty Walls of *Jericho* fell flat down to the Earth, and the *Ifraelites* enter'd the fame, and put to the Sword every Man, Woman and Child; and all Sorts of Cattle, and burnt the City to Afhes; only fparing the Harlot *Rahab*; and her Family, according to the Promife of the Spies, whom fhe had preferved from the Rage of the Men of *Jericho*, who fought to take away their Lives.

The HISTORY *of the* BIBLE

Circumcision renewed Iosh: 5 : 3

The Ark. of y̆ Covenant Iosh: 6:4.

Iosh: 5:3. And Ioshua made him sharp
knives and circumcised y̆ children &c
Iosh: 6:4. And seven priests shall bear
before y̆ ark 7 trumpets of rams &c

Fiue Kings hanged Iosua: 10: 26.

Gideon's present. Iudges 7: 20.

10:26 And afterward Iosua smot
and slew them and hanged y^m &c:
6:20: And y^e angell of God said unto
him take y^e flesh and y^e unleavened
&c:

XXXIII.
Five KINGS *hanged.*

JOSHUA purfuing his Victories. Five Kings, to wit, the King of *Jerufalem*, the King of *Hebron*, the King of *Jarmuth*, the King of *Lachifh*, and the King of *Eglon*, joined their Forces, to attack *Gibeon*, a City in Alliance with the *Ifraelites*, who thereupon joined Battle with the Five Kings ; and the Lord rained Hailftones upon their Enemies, and, at the Prayer of *Jofhua*, caufed the Sun and Moon to ftand ftill for three Days, till they were wholly difcomfitted ; and the Five Kings taking Refuge in a Cave at *Makkadah*, *Jofhua* commanded them to be brought forth, and having caufed his Officers to put their Feet on their Necks, in Token of the Lord's fubjecting their Enemies beneath their Feet, he fmote them and flew them, and hanged them on Five Trees, till the Evening, when their Bodies were taken down, and thrown into the Cave where they had hid themfelves, clofing up the Mouth thereof with great Stones.

XXXIV.
GIDEON*'s Prefent.*

AFTER the Death of *Jofhua*, and of that whole Generation, the Children of *Ifrael* fuffered themfelves to be feduced by the Heathens among whom they lived, to worfhip their falfe Gods and forfook that gracious God, who had heaped fo many miraculous favours upon them. Wherefore the Lord gave them into the Hands of the *Midianites*, who oppreffedd them fo exceedingly, that they crying to the Lord, he raifed up *Gideon* to deliver them ; to whom an Angel appearing, accepted of his Prefent of a Kid, and other Provifions, which he caufed him to put on a Rock, and made fire to come out of the Rock, by touching the Flefh with his Staff, which confumed the Flefh, and all the Provifions, *&c.*

XXXV. GIDEON's *Fleece*.

GIDEON being confirmed by this Miracle, that the Lord had chosen him to deliver his Country, destroy'd the Altar of *Baal*, which belonged to his Father *Joash*; at which the *Midianites* being incensed, drew up a mighty Army of several Nations, to revenge their false God, and to punish *Gideon*, who, by this Time, being followed by many *Israelites*, had raised a little Army against them. *And* Gideon *said unto God, if thou wilt save* Israel, *by my Hand, as thou hast said, I will put a Fleece of Wool in tie Floor, and if the Dew be on the Fleece only, and it be dry upon all the Earth beside, then shall I know that thou wilt save* Israel *by my Hand, as thou hast said. And it was so : for he rose up early on the Morrow, and thrust the Fleece together, and wringed the Dew out of the Fleece a Bowl-full of Water. And* Gideon *said unto God, Let not thine Anger be hot against me — Let it now be dry only upon the Fleece, and upon all the Ground let there be Dew. And God did so that Night.*

XXXVI. GIDEON's *Army*.

GIDEON being thus encouraged, encamped with his Army, which by this Time was increased to 32000 Men : But the Lord ordered him to proclaim, that whosoever was afraid, should quit the Army, lest the *Israelites* should vaunt, that their own Numbers had saved them ; and thereupon 22000 Men retired to their own Homes ; but the Lord still thinking the remaining 10000 too many, ordered *Gideon* to carry them down to the Water, and to chuse only those that lapped Water as a Dog, and not those that bowed down on their Knees to drink ; which reducing their Number to 300 Men, who were all that lapped, with these God miraculously was pleased to deliver his People, and destroy at one time 120,000 of the *Midianites*, together with *Oreb* and *Zeeb*, and *Zeba* and *Zalmunna*, Princes and Kings of *Midian*, and thereby intirely deliver'd *Israel* from the *Midianitish* Yoke.

The HISTORY *of the* BIBLE. 37

Gedeon's Fleece Iudg: 6:37

Gideon's army Iudg: 6:5:

6. 27. Behold I will put a fleece of wooll, in the floor and if the dew
7:5 So he brougt down the people unto y̌ water, and y̌ Lord said &c

Iepthah & his daughter Iud:11 39

Their Sacrifices

11:39. And it came to passe at y end of two months, that she returned to her Father who did with her according to his vow which he had vowed, &c.

XXXVII.
JEPHTHAH's *Vow*.

NEVER was People so much favoured by God, as the *Jews*, and never was there a more perverse and undeserving Nation ; in their Prosperity, always forsaking God, and never, but in Adversity, observing his Statutes. After the Death of *Gideon*, they returned to gross Idolatry ; so that the Lord raised up against them the numerous Armies of the *Ammonites*, which struck such a Consternation thro' *Israel*, that once more they laid aside their abominations, and turned to the Lord : who mercifully raised up *Jephthah* the *Gileadite* to defend them : This valiant Captain vowed a Vow, that if the Lord would deliver his Enemies into his Hands, he would offer for a Burnt Offering whatever came first out of his House to meet him ; and having totally discomfitted the *Ammonites*, on his returning in Triumph, his Daughter and only Child, came out to meet him with Timbrels and Dances.

XXXVIII.
JEPHTHAH's *Sacrifice*.

NOTHING could be more afflicting than this Sight to *Jephthah*, which turned all his Triumph into Mourning. He acquainted his Beloved Daughter with his Vow : who with, admirable Resignation, submitted to it, and besought him not to depart from it, because of his Tenderness to her desiring only, that she might be permitted to go upon the Mountans with her Female Companions, for the Space of two Months, to bewail her Virginity. Which *Jephthah* complying with, at the End of that Time she returned ; *And he did with her according to his Vow which he vowed. And it was a Custom in* Israel, *after that the Daughters of* Israel *went yearly to lament the Daughter of* Jephthah *four Days in a Year.*

XXXIX. MANOAH's *Sacrifice.*

AFTER the Death of *Jephthah*, the *Israelites* were govern'd by several other Judges, till doing Evil again in the Sight of the Lord, he gave them into the Hands of the *Philistines* for the Space of 40 Years. But at last being moved by their Oppressions and Repentance, he was pleased to raise up *Samson* for their Assistance. His Father's Name was *Manoah* of the Tribe of *Dan*, whose Wife having continued barren for many Years, an Angel appeared to her alone, and told her she should bear a Son, who should begin to deliver *Israel* from the *Philistines*: She not knowing it to be an Angel, informed her Husband of the Prediction, who praying to God also to see the Holy Man, the Angel appeared to them both, and renewed his Prediction; and commanded them to offer a Burnt-offering to the Lord (instead of paying any Honours to himself) he ascended up before them, in the Smoke thereof, leaving them both fully convinced of his Angelick Mission, and in a great Consternation at so extraordinary an Occurrence.

XL. SAMSON *killeth a Lyon.*

SAMSON, according to the Prediction of the Angel, being born and growing a Man, he cast his Eyes on a young Woman at *Timnah*, of the Daughters of the *Philistines*, whom he desired his Father and Mother to procure for his Wife. *Manoah* opposed his Choice at first, because she was a *Philistine*; but finding his Son insist upon it, he and his Wife accompanied him to *Timnah*, and as *Samson* was at some Distance from them in their Way, *Behold a young Lyon roared against him. And the Spirit of the Lord came mightily upon him, and he rent the Lyon as he would have rent a Kid, and he had nothing in his Hand; but he told not his Father nor his Mother what he hath done*: But proceeded on his Way, and gaining the Consent of the young Woman and her Parents, a Day was fix'd for his Espousals.

Monoah's Sacrifice Judg: 13:20

Samson killeth a Lion: 14:6.

13:20. For it came to passe when ỹ flame went up &c. towards heaven
14.6. And ỹ spirit of ỹ Lord came mightilie upon him &c:

Samson smiteth yͤ Philistines Iud: 15.15

Samson carrieth away yͤ Gates Iudg: 16:3

15:15: And he found a new jaw bone of
of an Asse, and put forth his hand &c.
16:3 And Samson lay till midnight and
arose, at midnight and tooke the &c

XLI. SAMSON *smiteth the* Philistines.

AS *Samson* returned to marry his Wife, he found in the Carcase of the dead Lyon, Bees, and Honey, which he eat of: And at his Wedding Feast propounded this Riddle to 30 young Men at the Table, *viz. Out of the Eater came forth Meat, and out of the Strong, Sweetness* ; promising them 30 Changes of Rayment, and 30 Sheets, if, within a fixed Time, they could expound the same provided, that if they could not, they should give him the same Reward. The set Time being almost elapsed, they prevailed on his Wife to get the Secret out of him : Which being revealed to them, so enraged *Samson*, that he flew 30 *Philistines*, and gave their Rayment to those who had expounded the Riddle. After this, in his Absence, his Wife being given to another Man, he caught 300 Foxes, and tied them Tail to Tail, with Firebrands between each, and letting them loose among the standing Corn of the *Philistines*, he consumed that and their Vineyards and Olives. This inraging the *Philistines*, they burnt his Wife and her Father ; whereupon *Samson* smote them Hip and Thigh, with a great Slaughter, and went and dwelt on the Top of a Rock. The *Philistines* being gathered together for Revenge, the Men of *Judah* persuaded Samson to let them bind him with new Cords, and deliver him up to the *Philistines*, who seeing him bound, gave a great Shout; upon which the Spirit of the Lord coming upon *Samson*, he snapt the new Cords as if they had been burnt Flax, and finding the Jaw Bone of an Ass, he fell upon the *Philistines*, and therewith slew 1000 Men.

XLII. Samson *carrieth away the Gates.*

AND it was told the Gazites, *saying,* Samson *is come hither. And they compassed him in, and laid wait for him, and having secured the Gates, were quiet all the Night, saying. In the Morning, when it is Day, we shall kill him : And* Samson *arose at Midnight, and took the Doors of the Gate of the City, the two Posts, Bar and all, and carried them up to the Top of an Hill that is before* Hebron.

XLIII. DELILAH's *Falshood*.

THE Lords of the *Philistines* having fought all Opportunities to be revenged of *Samson*, to no Purpose, at last had recourse to a Woman named *Delilah*, for whom he had a great Affection ; offering her mighty Rewards if she could prevail upon him to reveal where his great Strength lay. Three several Times he amused her with wrong Accounts, and so escaped the Snare laid for him : *But at length, When she pressed him daily with her Words, and urged him so, that his Soul was vexed unto Death, he told her all his Heart, and said unto her, There hath not come a Razor upon mine Head for I have been a* Nazarite *unto God from my Mother's Womb : If I be shaven, then my Strength will go from me, and I shall become weak, and be like any other Man.* Delilah hereupon making him sleep upon her Knees, sent for the Lords of the *Philistines*, and caused a Man to shave off the *Seven Locks of his Head, and his Strength went from him, and the* Philistines *took him, and put out his Eyes, and brought him down to* Gaza, *and bound him with Fetters of Brass, and he did grind in the Prison-house.* And thus was *Samson* severely punished for revealing his Secrets to a wicked Prostitute.

XLIV. SAMSON's *Revenge and Death*.

BUT in a little Time *Samson*'s Hair beginning to grow again, his Strength also returned : Mean while the *Philistines* triumphed exceedingly in their Conquest, and on a Time making a Sacrifice in Gratitude to their God *Dagon*, who they supposed had delivered their Enemy into their Hands, being very merry, they sent for *Samson* to make them Sport ; who being brought and placed between the Two Pillars that supported the House, he took one in each Hand, and calling upon God to assist him that once to revenge himself for his two Eyes, and desiring to die with them, *he bowed himself with all his might, and the House fell upon the Lords, and upon all the People that were therein : So the Dead which he slew at his Death, were wore than they which he slew in his Life.*

The HISTORY of the BIBLE   45

Delilah's falshood Iudg 16 19.

Samson's death Iudg: 16: 29.

16:19. And she made him sleep upon her
lap and she caled for a man and she &c
16.29 And Samson tooke hold of yͤ two
midle pillres upon which the house &c

Neomi & her two daughters. 1:8
Ruth. 1.2.3.4

Boaz and Ruth   2:c: 8.v.

8 And Naomi said unto her two
daughters in law, Go return &c:
2:8 Then said Boaz unto Ruth
hearest thou not my daughter &c

XLV. Naomi *and her two Daughters.*

NAOMI having buried her Husband and Two Sons in the Land of *Moab*, whither they had retired when there was a Famine in the Land of *Judah*, and being difpofed to return to her own Country, which was again bleffed with Plenty, fhe endeavour'd to perfuade *Orpah* and *Ruth*, the Widows of her deceafed Sons, to leave her in her Misfortunes, and return to their Mother's Houfe, where they would probably be lefs expofed to the Hardfhips her Poverty and Affliction muft needs involve them in : *Orpah* was mov'd by her Arguments, and took leave of her Mother; but *Ruth*, having more Piety, and a ftronger Faith in God's Providence, faid to *Naomi*, *Intreat me not to leave thee, or return from following after thee ; for whither thou goeft I will go, and where thou lodgeft I will lodge : Thy People fhall be my People, and thy God my God : Where thou dieft will I die, and there will I be buried. The Lord do fo to me, and more alfo, if ought but Death part thee and me.* *Naomi* feeing fhe was ftedfaftly refolved, defifted from her Perfuafions; and *they two went until they were come to* Bethlehem.

XLVI. BOAZ's *Kindnefs to* Ruth.

IT was the Beginning of Barley-harveft, when *Naomi* and *Ruth* arrived at *Bethlehem*, and *Ruth* going to glean in the Fields of *Boaz*, a very wealthy Relation of *Naomi*'s late Husband, *Boaz* caft his Eyes upon her, and being informed who fhe was, he applauded her dutiful Behaviour to her Mother-in-Law, and enjoin'd her to glean in no other Field but his, during the whole Time of Harveft ; and to keep faft by his Maidens ; and after fhe was gone to glean, he order'd his Servants that they fhould drop Handfuls on purpofe for her to take up ; which they did, infomuch, that when fhe had beat out that fhe had gleaned, it was about an Ephah of Barley.

XLVII.
RUTH *lieth at the Feet of* BOAZ.

NAOMI rejoicing at *Boaz*'s kindness to her Daughter-in-Law, and being willing to improve his favourable Disposition to her, commanded *Ruth* to watch the Place of his Repose in the Threshing-floor, where he was to winnow Barley that Night, and when he was laid down, and was fallen asleep, to uncover his Feet, and to lay herself down by him. *Ruth* obey'd, and being laid down by him, he awoke at Midnight, and was at first surprized to find a Woman at his Feet; but *Ruth* revealing herself, and claiming of him the Right of marrying her, according to the *Jewish* Custom, as being her near Kinsman, he applauded her Choice, in that she had not set her Heart on a young, indiscreet Man, and told her, that there was still a nearer Relation than he, of whom he would require to perform the Duty of nearest Kinsman, and if he declined it, he himself would marry her. And in the Morning presenting her with six Measures of Barley, he dismissed her, with much Civility and Kindness.

XLVIII.
BOAZ *married* RUTH.

BOAZ rested not till he made good his Promise to *Ruth*, and having, as was the Custom, required, publickly, the nearest Kinsman to marry *Ruth*, and he having declin'd it, *Boaz* took Witnesses of it, and espoused her himself: And in .process of Time she conceived and bore a Son, who was called *Obed*, who was the Father of *Jesse* the Father of King David, from which Stock, according to the Flesh, afterwards descended our blessed Lord and Saviour *Jesus Christ*. And thus gloriously, for an Example to all Children, was *Ruth* rewarded for her filial Duty to her Mother-in-Law.

Ruth lieth at Boaz's feet. 3:7

He marieth her 4:9

3:7 And when Boaz had eaten &
drunk and his heart was merry &c
4:9 And Boaz said unto the elders
and unto all the people &c.

Samuel killeth Agag. 1 Sam: 15: 33

David killeth Goliah. 1 Sam: 17: 51.

And Samuell said as thy sword hath
made women childlesse, so shall &c.
Therefore David ran and stood

XLIX. SAMUEL *killeth* AGAG.

THE *Ifraelites* having requefted of the Prophet *Samuel*, that he would make them a King to judge them like other Nations, the Lord was pleafed to comply with their Requeft, and directed Samuel to anoint for their King, *Saul* the Son of *Kifh* who having, by the Divine Affiftance, fubdued many powerful Nations, was at laft commanded to fall upon the Amalekites, and to fpare neither Man, Woman nor Child, nor Ox, Sheep, Camel nor Afs ; Saul accordingly made great Slaughter of the *Amalekites* ; but took Prifoner King *Agag* their King, whom he fpared, and alfo the beft of their Cattle, from a Principle of Avarice : Whereupon *Samuel* having feverely rebuked *Saul* for not fulfilling the Command of the Lord, and threatned him with the Deprivation of his Kingdom, he ordered *Agag* to be brought forth, whom he hewed in Pieces before the Lord in *Gilgai*.

L. DAVID *killeth* GOLIATH.

GOD being difpleafed with *Saul*, determined to transfer the Kingdom from him to *David*, the Great Grandfon of *Boaz* and *Ruth* : Nor was it long before an Occafion offer'd to fignalize this Youth in the Face of all *Ifrael*; for a mighty Champion of the *Philiftines* called *Goliath* of *Gath*, who was Six Cubits and a Span high, and of prodigious Strength, having defy'd the Champions of *Ifrael* for 40 Days, ftruck fuch a Terror into them, that they always fled at the Sight of him, as often as he appear'd. With this mighty Champion *David*, tho a Stripling, undertook to encounter, notwithstanding the Perfuafions and Apprehenfions of the whole Camp ; and having taken his Sling he went to meet him, and flung a Stone that entered the *Philiftine*'s Forehead, and felled him flat to the Earth ; whereupon *David* ran and ftood upon him, and with his own Sword ftruck off his Head, which occafioned the total Difcomfiture of the *Philiftines*.

LI.

SAUL envieth DAVID.

THIS extraordinary victory obtained by *David*, having gain'd him the Applause and Affection of the People, *Saul* grew jealous of him, and determined to destroy him ; and being troubled with an Evil Spirit from the Lord, David was used to play upon his Harp, which diverted his Melancholy, and caused the Evil Spirit to depart from him : And on a Time, as *David* was playing on his Harp to divert him, *Saul*, having a Javelin in his Hand, *cast the Javelin for he said, I will smite* David *even to the Wall with it; and* David *avoided out of his Presence twice.*

LII.

JONATHAN's Kindness to DAVID.

BUT tho *David* had the Misfortune to incur the Displeasure of *Saul*, yet his great Merits attached to him *Jonathan Saul*'s Son ; who loved him as his own Soul, and gave him Notice from Time to Time of all the Evil intended to him by his Father. And the Feast of the New Moon being at Hand, when it was usual for all the Courtiers to attend the King, and *David* not daring to be present for fear of being put to Death, it was agreed upon between them, That if *Jonathan* should discover that his Father intended Mischief to *David*, he would shoot his Arrows near a Place in the Field where David was to be hid, and if he bid his Boy fetch them from beyond him, and not on this Side of him ; that then he should make his Escape. And *Jonathan* having found his Father's Resolution to destroy *David*, he shot his Arrows beyond him as was agreed, and *David* made the best of his Way, having first sworn to a strict Covenant with *Jonathan*.

The HISTORY of the BIBLE

Saul envieth him. I Sam: 18:11

Ionathan's kindneſs. I Sam: 20:35

And Saul caſt y̆ Iaudin for he said, I
will ſmite David even to the wall &
And it came to paſſe in y̆ morning y̆
Ionathan went out into y̆ feild &c:

Nabal's churlishness. 1 Sam. 25:10

Abigail's wisdom 1 Sam. 25:18

25:10 And Naball answered Davids servants, and said who is David &c.
25:18 Then Abigail made hast and took 200 loaves and 2 botles of wine &c

LIII. NABAL's *Churlishness*.

DAVID being obliged to flee into the Wilderness to avoid *Saul*'s Resentment, he became a Captain over several Hundreds of Persons who resorted to him to avoid their Creditors, or some other Distress, and hearing that *Nabal*, a mighty rich Man, whose Shepherds he had protected in *Carmel*, was Shearing his Sheep there, he sent ten of his Followers to him to remind him of his Civility to his Servants, and desire him to send him some Provisions or whatsoever he could spare. But *Nabal* being *churlish and evil in his Doings, answered* David's *Servants, and said, Who is* David *? And who is the Son of* Jesse *? There be many Servants now-a-days that break away every Man from his Master. Shall I then take my Bread and my Water, and my Flesh that I have kill'd for my Shearers, and give it unto Men whom I know not whence they be ?* So David's *young Men went again, and told him all those Sayings.*

LIV. ABIGAIL's *Wisdom*.

DAVID being exasperated at this churlish Answer, ordered all his Followers to gird on their Swords, and vowed by the Morning Light to leave not a Man alive of all *Nabal*'s Family. But the Servants of *Nabal* fearing what might happen, went to their Master's Wife *Abigail*, and informed her of their Apprehensions, and of the Civilities they had received at *David*'s Hands ; who thereupon took 200 Loaves and two Bottles of Wine, and five Sheep ready dress'd, with other Provisions, and having loaden several Asses, with them she set out with divers of her Servants, unknown to her Husband, and met *David* on full March with his Men in order to destroy *Nabal*'s House and Family : But being appeased by her graceful Demeanour and Humility, he receiv'd her and her Presents kindly, and was diverted from his Purpose ; And *Abigail* being very beautiful as well as discreet and *Nabal* dying for Vexation when he was told what had happened, *David* took her to Wife.

LV. The WITCH of Endor.

WHILE Matters went thus with *David*, *Samuel* the Prophet died, and *Saul* having in vain purfued *David* from Place to Place, and finding the Lord had left him, and being terrified at the great Armies of the *Philiftines* which were drawn up againft him, he went to a Woman who had a familiar Spirit, and defired her to bring up *Samuel*, which having done, he requir'd of him what he fhould do in his Diftrefs? *Samuel* affur'd him, That the Lord had rent his Kingdom from him, and given it to *David*, and that on the next Day, God would deliver him and the *Ifraelites* with him, into the Hands of the *Philiftines*; and that he and his Sons fhould be with him in Death. This terrible Prediction fo affected Saul, that he fell *ftraitway all along on the Earth, and there was no Strength in him*; and when he recover'd, he would neither be comforted nor refrefh'd.

LVI. SAUL's *Death*.

ACcording to the Prophet's Prediction, the next Day both Armies having engag'd on Mount *Gilboa*, the *Ifraelites* were difcomfited, and *Saul*'s Sons *Jonathan*, *Ahinadab* and *Malchifna*, being flain, and himfelf fore wounded, he faid unto his Armour-bearer, Draw thy Sword and thruft me through therewith, left thefe Uncircumcifed come and thruft me through, and abufe me. But his Armour-bearer refufing, *Saul* took a Sword and fell upon it; which when his Armour-bearer faw, he likewife fell upon his Sword, and died with him. And when the *Philiftines* found *Saul* among the Slain; they cut off his Head, fent his Armour to *Afhtaroth*, and faftened his Body to the Walls of *Bethfhan*, together with the Bodies of his Sons; which afterward were refcued from them by the Inhabitants of *Jabefh Gilead*, who decently interr'd their Bodies. And David extreamly lamented the Lofs of *Saul*, and more efpecially of his beloved Friend *Jonathan*.

The HISTORY *of the* BIBLE 57

The witch of Endor 1 Sam: 28:8.

Saul's death & his armour bearer

28:8 *And Saul disguised him:selfe
and put on other rayment and &c:*
31:4 *Then said Saul to his armour
bearer draw thy sword and &c:*

Bethsheba's request. 1 Kings. 2. 20:

He seats his mother on his right hand 2:22

2:20. Then she said I desire one small petition of thee I pray thee say me not
2:22: And why doest thou aske Abishag ye Shunamite for Adonijah &c

LVII.

BATHSHEBA's *Request*.

AFTER this deplorable fate of *Saul* and his House, God was pleased to establish the Throne of *David* over *Israel* and *Judah*, and to deliver his Enemies into his Hand. And David having reigned forty Years, appointed his Son *Solomon* his Successor, preferably to his eldest Son *Adonijah*, and died in a good old Age. When *Adonijah* perceived all his Efforts to succeed to his Father, of no avail, he gave way to his Brother's good Fortune; but meditating to strengthen his Pretensions to the Throne, he desired *Bathsheba*, the Mother of King *Solomon*, to request the King to grant him to Wife *Abishag* the *Shunammite*, a beautiful Damsel, who had cherished King *David*, and ministred unto him, and lay in his Bosom, when, he was so old, that no Heat could be kept in him. *Bathsheba* courteously undertook the Message; not being aware of his Design in it, and went to her Son, the King, to request this Favour of him.

LVIII.

His seats his Mother on his Right-Hand.

AS soon as the King beheld his Mother, he dutifully rose to meet her, and causing her to be plac'd on the Throne on his Right Hand, he sat down by her, and promised to grant whatever she should desire of him: But when he heard her request, *He answered and said, And why dost thou ask* Abishag *the* Shunammite *for* Adonijah? *Ask for him the Kingdom also* —— *Then King* Solomon *sware by the Lord, saying, God do so to me and more also, if* Adonijah *have not spoken this Word against his own Life. Now therefore as the Lord liveth,* Adonijah *shall be put to Death this Day!*

LIX. ADONIJAH *slain.*

SOLOMON, as he had sworn, accordingly sent *Benaiah* the Son of *Jehoida*, who was his chief Captain, and he fell upon *Adonijah* and slew him : He after this removed *Abiathar*, a Friend of *Adonijah*, from being Chief *Priest*, putting *Zadock* one of his own Followers, into his Place ; and not long after, caused the same *Benaiah* to fall upon the valiant *Joab*, who had been David's chief General, and to slay him at the Horns of the Altar which he had taken hold of for a Sanctuary, he having also been attach'd to *Adonijah* as the eldest Son of his Royal Master. By these Removes and Sacrifices, so customary with Princes whose Crowns are contested, and especially with the Princes of the *East*, did *Solomon* establish his Throne over *Israel*.

LX. SOLOMON*'s Judgment.*

SOLOMON having requested *Wisdom* of the Lord, preferably to either *Riches* or *Power*, the Lord was pleased to add them all to him, and to promise him Wisdom beyond all those who went before him, or that should come after him. It happened an extraordinary Case came before him soon after, which redounded greatly to his Reputation ; for two Harlots living in one House by themselves, and being both brought to Bed within three Days of each other, the Child of one of them dying, the Mother changed the dead one for the live one, while the other was asleep, and insisted strongly that it was her own. This Case coming before the King, and both claiming the living Child, *Solomon* order'd that it should be divided with a Sword between them : To this the pretended Mother assenting, the true one, besought the King to let the other have it whole, rather than to destroy her Child ; which at once shew'd she was the true Mother, and ended the Controversy.

Adonijah slain 2:25.

Solomon's Iudgment. 3:16:

2.25: And king Solomon sent by ye hand of Benaiah ye son of Ie
3:16 Then came there two women that were harlots unto the king &

The Temple begun. I Kings. 6:2.

Solomon's prayer I Kings. 8:23

6:2 And ye house wch King Solomon built for the Lord, the length thereof &c
8:23. And he said Lord God of Israell there is no god like thee in heaven &c

LXI.

The TEMPLE *begun,*

GOD having reserved to the peaceable Reign of *Solomon*, the Building of a Temple to his Honour, that Prince set about the important Work, which when built and finish'd, became the Glory of the City of *Jerusalem*, and one of the seven Wonders of the World. For its Dimensions, curious Workmanship, and the Richness of its Utensils and Ornaments, we must refer our Readers to the Description given of it in sacred Writ, 1 *Kings*, vi, vii. having not Room, in this small Compass, to describe its wonderful Splendor, Magnificence, and Beauty.

LXII.

SOLOMON*'s Prayer.*

SOLOMON having finish'd this glorious Fabrick, assembled the Elders of all *Israel*, and caused the Ark of the Lord to be carried into an Apartment peculiarly allotted for its Residence, by far the most rich and splendid of the whole Building, called the *Holy of Holies*; and having sacrificed 22,000 Oxen, and 120,000 Sheep, he dedicated the Temple to the Lord, and blessed the People, and made a solemn Prayer to the Almighty, acknowledging his Power and his Mercies and begging first a Blessing upon himself and his House, he besought the Lord to hearken to the Cries of his People, whensoever they should offer their Supplications towards that Place, and to forgive them their Offences, and assist them in all their Distresses and Exigences: After which he hallow'd the Temple, and made a Feast for all *Israel*, which lasted 14 Days, and then dismissed the People. *And they Blessed the King, and went into their Tents joyful and glad of Heart, for all the Goodness that the Lord had done for* David *his Servant, and for* Israel *his People.*

LXIII. SOLOMON's *Magnificence*.

NOW *King* Solomon *exceeded all the Kings of the Earth for Riches and for Wisdom ; and he made a great Throne of Ivory, and overlaid it with the best Gold ; The Throne had six Steps,* and twelve Lyons were placed, six on each side of the Steps, and two Lyons beside the Stays of it ; *there was not the like made in any Kingdom. And when the Queen of Sheba heard of his Fame, she came to prove him with hard Questions,* attended with a great Train, and laden with Spices, and Gold, and precious Stones, as Presents to him ; and when she had seen his magnificent Buildings, his splendid Court, and all his Wisdom, *there was no more Spirit in her* ; and she acknowledged that the Report of his Glory and his Fame, which had induced her to leave her own Country to be Witness of them, and which 'till now she had scarce believed, was far short of what she had beheld ; and pronouncing his Servants happy, who every Day heard his Wisdom, and blessing the Lord for his Mercies to him, she returned to her own Country loaden with magnificent Presents made her by King *Solomon*.

LXIV. SOLOMON's *Idolatry*.

THE Frailty of human Nature was never more conspicuous in any Man than in King *Solomon*, and shews what weak Creatures the best and wisest of Men are, when left to themselves, or when they give the Reigns to their headstrong Passions. After all the Blessings of the Almighty heaped upon this great Prince, he suffer'd himself, in his old Age, to be drawn away to worship strange Gods, by his Wives, whom to the Number of 700, besides 300 Concubines, he had taken from the Idolatrous Nations round him, which the Lord had commanded the *Israelites* not to inter-marry with : For this his Iniquity, the Lord threatned to rend away ten Tribes, and leave only one to his Son, and that for his Father *David*'s Sake : On whose Account also he promised not to do this in *Solomon*'s Life-Time.

Solomon's Magnificence 1 Kings 10:1

His offering to y̆ Idol. 1 Kings. 11:4.

10:1 And y̆ queen of Sheba heard of y̆
fame of Solomon concerning &c
11:4 For it came to passe when Solomō
was old that his wives turned away &c

DAVID

SOLOMON

David king and Prophet author
of the Psalmes and reigned 40 y:rs
Solomon reigned in Ierusalem and
over all Israell fortie yeares

LXV.
King DAVID.

THE Four moſt celebrated Kings of *Judah* were *David*, *Solomon* his Son, *Jehoſhaphat*, and King *Joſiah*. DAVID, as we Have related, was the Son of *Jeſſe*, raiſed by the Lord to ſucceed to *Saul* and his Family. He was a Prince of great Valour and Wiſdom, an excellent Poet and Prophet, and called a *Man after God's own Heart* : To him are the greateſt Part of the Book of *Pſalms* aſcribed : He ſubdu'd the Enemies of *Iſrael*, and after having reigned Forty Years, died in a good old Age, leaving his Crown and Kingdom to his Son *Solomon*.

LXVI.
King SOLOMON.

SOLOMON was the greateſt and moſt magnificent, as well as the wifeſt King, that ever reigned. He was the Author of the Books of *Proverbs*, *Eccleſiaſtes*, and the *Canticles*, called the *Song of Solomon*. The Scripture is thus expreſs relating to his Works ; *As ſpake 3000 Proverbs, and his Songs were a Thouſand and Five* : He ſpake of Trees from the Cedar that is in Lebanon, even unto tie Hyſſop that ſpringeth out of the Wall. He ſpake alſo of Beaſts, and of Fowl, and of creeping Things, and of Fiſhes ; which Book is ſuppoſed to be loſt in the Deſtruction of the glorious Temple erected by him. He alſo reigned Forty Years, and left his Kingdom to his Son *Rehoboam*.

LXVII.

King JEHOSHAPHAT.

JEHOSHAPHAT was the son *Asa*, King of *Judah*, and succeeded his Father at the Age of 35 Years, and reigned 25, with the greatest Splendor and Magnificence. He was a Prince of great Piety and Goodness, and God subjected all his Enemies under his Feet, and caused the numerous Armies of *Moab, Mount-Seir*, and the Children of *Ammon*, who had joined together against him, to fall upon one another, and totally destroy themselves, without a Blow from *Jehoshaphat*. This Prince walking in the Ways of God, the Almighty was pleased so to bless him with Prosperity and Riches in abundance; and his Armies were so powerful, that he had Eleven Hundred and Sixty Thousand Men of Valour ready upon all Occasions.

LXVIII.

King JOSIAH.

JOSIAH was eight years old when he began to reign, and was a Prince of extraordinary Piety and Goodness, so that the Scripture testifies of him, *That like unto him was there no King that turned to the Lord with all his Heart, and with all his Soul, and with all his Might, according to all the Law of Moses; neither after him arose there any like him.* He destroyed all the High Places that had been built to Baal, and rooted Idolatry out of the Land. But he had not equal Success against his Enemies; the Lord, for the Sins of the People and of his Predecessors, suffering him to be slain in a Battle by *Pharaoh Necho* King of *Ægypt*, after he had reigned 31 Years in *Jerusalem*.

IEHOSHAPHAT

IOSIAS

Iehoshaphat reigned 5 and 20
yeares & congered ye Amonits
Iosias wighned 31 yeares he demo-
lished Idols and brought in ye

Ahijah's prophesy. 1 Kings: 11: 29:

Rehoboam consults ye old Men

11:29 And it came to passe at that time
when Ieroboam went out of Ierusa: or
12:6 And King Rehoboam consulted
with ye old men that stood before &c.

LXIX. ABIJAH's *Prophesy*.

WE shall now pursue the History of *Solomon*, who, as we have related, suffer'd himself to be seduced by his Wives to Idolatry. This his Depravity so provoked the Almighty, that he raised him up several powerful Enemies, and among the rest *Jeroboam* the Son of *Nebat*, who was a Man of great Valour, and one of his own Officers. It happened on a Time, that this Person being cloathed with a new Garment, and being gone out of *Jerusalem*, the Prophet *Abijah* the *Shilonite* met him in the Field, and taking hold of his new Garment, he rent it in 12 Pieces, giving ten of them to Jeroboam, and declaring to him, that after *Solomon*'s Death, the Lord would in like manner rend 10 Tribes from the Hands of his Son, and give them to him, as a Punishment for *Solomon*'s Sin of Idolatry; and at the same Time promising to establish *Jeroboam*'s Kingdom over *Israel*, if he walked in the Way of the Lord. After this *Jeroboam* fled into *Ægypt*, to avoid the Wrath of *Solomon*, who would have killed him, to frustrate *Abijah*'s Prophesy.

LXX. *King* REHOBOAM.

SOLOMON being dead, his Son Rehoboam of human was made King in his stead; and as soon as *Jeroboam* heard this, he came from *Ægypt* to *Jerusalem* and joining himself to the Congregation of *Israel*, they petition'd the King for a Redress of the Grievances that had crept into the Government in the latter Part of his Father's Reign; rendring their Duty and Service to him, if he would make their Burthens lighter. Upon this, the King consulted with his old Counsellors, who advised him to sooth their inflam'd Passions, and to promise them a Redress of their Grievances, in order to secure their Faith and Allegiance to him, at the Beginning of his Reign.

LXXI.

REHOBOAM *confulteth the young Men.*

BUT this young Prince, being vainly puffed up with his new Dignity, would not condefcend to footh the Paffions of the People; but adhered to the Advice of Perfons of his own Age and Inexperience, the Companions and Favourites of his Youth, who perfuaded him, that it was moft becoming of the Royal Dignity, to threaten and terrify the People into their Duty, rather than to appear to comply in the leaft with their Petitions: Being of the Opinion of thofe Court Parafites and Flatterers, who would perfuade young Princes, to their Ruin, That the People were made for Slaves to the Prince, and born with Saddles on their Backs; and that a Monarch had no more to do, but get up and ride: Which Advice many indifcreet Princes, both before and fince *Rehoboam*, have fo far purfu'd, 'till the oppreffed People, being tyr'd with their Burthens, have rifen as one Man, and caft their unkingly Rider: As proved to be the Cafe with this mifled Prince.

LXXII.

REHOBOAM *threatneth the People*

JEROBOAM and the Elders of the People, attending the King at the appointed Time for an Anfwer to their Petitions, this rafh Prince, according to the Advice of his young Counfellors, anfwered them roughly, faying, *My Father made your Yoke heavy, and I will add to your yoke: My Father alfo chaftized you with Whips, but I will chaftize you with Scorpions.* This Anfwer inraging the People, they cry'd out, *What Portion have we in David?* —— *To your Tents*, O Ifrael! *Now fee to thine own Houfe*, David! And immediately departing, 10 Tribes fell off from the Houfe of *David*, and chofe *Jeroboam* for their King, according to the Word of *Abijah* the Prophet.

The HISTORY *of the* BIBLE 73

Rehoboam Consults y̆ young men
71

Rehoboam threatneth y̆ People 12:14
72

12:9. *And he said unto them what*
counsell giue ye, that y̆ may &c:
12:14. *And spake unto them after the*
counsell

Elijah prophi.^t against Ahab 1 Kng 17:1

Elijah and y^e Widow of Zerephath

17:1 And Elijah y^e Tishbite, who was of the inhabitants of Gilliad said unto Ahab &c.
17:9 Arise and get thee to Zerephath which belongeth to Zedon and &c.

LXXIII. ELIJAH *prophesies against* AHAB.

VARIOUS were the Revolutions that afterwards follow'd in the Kingdom of *Israel*, which Jeroboam had founded: For he doing Evil in the Sight of the Lord, and erecting Altars to two Golden Calves which he set up to divert the People, for Political Reasons, from going to worship the Lord at *Jerusalem*, the Lord was pleased to cut of all his House and Family by the Hand of *Baasha*; who also doing Evil in the Sight of the Lord, the Lord destroy'd all his House and Family by the Hand of *Zimri*; who burning himself to Death to avoid the Punishment due to his Treason, *Omri* ascended the Throne, and after a Reign of 22 Years, died, and was succeeded by his Son *Ahab*, who was a greater Idolater and a wickeder Man, than all that went before him: Insomuch, that the great Prophet *Elijah* prophesy'd against him, and assured him, that there mould not be Dew or Rain in *Israel* for Years to come, but according to his Word.

LXXIV. Elijah *and the Widow of Zarephath*.

ELIJAH, after this by the Command of the Lord, hid himself by the Brook *Cherith*, and the Lord caused the Ravens to bring him Bread and Flesh both Morning and Evening. Afterwards by the Divine Command, he went to a Widow at *Zarephath*, whom he found gathering Sticks, in order to make a Fire to dress a little Meat, which, with a small Cruse of Oil, was all the Sustenance she had for herself and Son; as she told the Prophet, when he desir'd a little Bread and Water at her Hands: But *Elijah* commanded her notwithstanding, to bring him a little Cake, and promis'd her, that her Barrel of Meal and Cruse of Oil should not fail, till God sent Rain upon the Earth: Which was accordingly fulfilled, and they all three were sustain'd many Days by this small Pittance, which the good Widow thought would hardly serve for one Meal for her self and Son.

LXXV. Elijah *reproveth* Ahab.

THE Widow's Son sickening after this, and dying, the Lord was pleased, at the Supplications of the Prophet, to restore him to Life, to the great Joy of the poor Widow, who before that was inconsolable for his Loss, and in her Agony of Sorrow, imputed his Death to the Presence of *Elijah*. And in the third Year after the great Drought, the Lord commanded *Elijah* to go shew himself to *Ahab*, promising to send Rain upon the Earth : *Ahab* in the mean while, had caused search to be made for *Elijah*, throughout *Israel*, in order to slay him, imputing to him the Famine which then sorely raged in *Samaria*, and as soon as he saw the Prophet, he sternly said, *Art then he that troubleth* Israel? *And he answered, I have not troubled* Israel, *but thou and thy Father's House, in that ye have forsaken the Commandments of the Lord, And thou hast followed* Baalim.

LXXVI. Elijah *'s Sacrifice.*

ELIJAH then, in order to convince *Ahab* of the Folly of his Idolatry, persuaded him to assemble the 450 Prophets of *Baal*, and cause them to offer a Sacrifice to *Baal* of a Bullock, cut in Pieces, and he would do the same to the Lord, and the God who should answer by Fire from Heaven on the Sacrifice, should be acknowledged the only true God. *Baal*'s Priests could not refuse the Tryal, and called upon *Baal* from Morning till Evening, in the most violent Transports of superstitious Zeal, to no Purpose. And Elijah in his Turn, having caused a Trench to be made, and 12 Barrels of Water to be pour'd on the Wood and on the Sacrifice, till the Trench was filled, he supplicated the Almighty to assert his Power to the Conviction of those Idolaters, and in the Sight of the King and all the People, Fire descended from Heaven, *and consumed the Burnt Sacrifice, and the Wood, and the Stones, and the Dust, and licked up the Water, that was in the Trench.*

Elijah reproveth Ahab i King: 18:18

Elijah Sacrificeth 1 Kings 18:38

18:18 And he answeed, I haue not troub
Israell, but thou and thy fathers house &c
18 38 And ỹ fire of ỹ Lord fell, and
consumed ỹ burnt Sacrifice &c.

Elijah in y^e Fiery Chariot II Kin:u

The Widow's oil II Kings 4:1

2:11. And it came to passe as they still went on and talked &c.
4:1 Now there cryed a certain woman of the wives of the sons of y^e &c

LXXVII.

ELIJAH *in the Fiery Chariot.*

AND *when all the People saw this, they fell on their Faces, and they said, The LORD he is the God! The LORD he is the God! And* Elijah *said unto them, Take the Prophets of* Baal, *let not one of them escape: And they took them, and* Elijah *brought them down to the Brook* Kiſhon, *and ſlew them there. And* Elijah *said unto* Ahab, *Get thee up, eat and drink ; for there is a Sound of Abundance of Rain* : Which accordingly came to paſs. This great Prophet having miraculouſly by the Aſſiſtance of God perform'd theſe and many other great Things to the Glory of the Almighty, and having appointed *Eliſha* to ſucceed him as a Prophet, according to the Divine Command, was at laſt taken up, in the Preſence of *Eliſha,* by a Chariot and Horſes of Fire, in a Whirlwind, to Heaven, and dropping his Mantle from him, *Eliſha* took it up, and with it divided the Waters of *Jordan,* and paſſed over dry-ſhod as he had ſeen *Elijah* do before.

LXXVII.

The WIDOW's Oil.

NOW there came a certain Woman unto Eliſha, *ſaying, Thy Servant my Husband is dead, and the Creditor is come to take unto him my two Sons to be Bondmen.* And *Eliſha* ſaid unto her, What ſhall I do for thee ? —— *What haſt thou in the houſe? And ſhe ſaid, Thine handmaid hath not any Thing in the Houſe, ſave a Pot of Oil.* Then he commanded her to borrow a great Number of Veſſels of her Neighbours, and pour out into thoſe Veſſels till they were full ; which ſhe did, and found ſo great a Quantity, that ſhe ſold a Part of it for as much as ſatisfy'd her Debts, and there was enough left to ſubſiſt her and her Children.

LXXIX. NAAMAN's *Leprosy cured.*

AFTER this, *Naaman* the *Syrian* General, who was a man of great Valor, but a Leper, hearing of Elisha's Miracles, went, nobly attended, to his House, to seek a Cure at his Hands: Whereupon Elijba sent him Word by a Servant, to wash seven Times in Jordan, and he should be clean. Naaman expecting to have seen Elisha himself, and that he should have been instantly cured by his Prayers to God for him went away in a great Rage, saying, are not the Rivers of *Damascus* of greater Virtue than the Waters of *Israel*? But being *persuaded* to comply with the Prophet's Advice, he went down to *Jordan*, and dipped himself seven Times ; and his Flesh came again, and he was clean. Upon which he confessed, that there was no God in all the Earth, but in *Israel* and offer'd great Presents to *Elisha*, who absolutely refused them ; and smote with *Naaman*'s Leprosy, his Servant *Gehazi*, who clandestinely, in his Master's Name, obtain'd some Presents for himself.

LXXX. JEZEBEL's *Death.*

AHAB having been slain by the *Syrians*, and the Lord having caused *Elisha* to anoint *Jehu* for King of *Israel*, with a Command to cut off all the House of *Ahab*, *Jehu* accordingly conspired against his Master King *Joram*, the Son of *Ahab*, and having killed him, he enter'd *Israel* in Triumph, and seeing the wicked *Jezebel*, *Ahab's* wife, at the Palace Window, who reproached him for his Conspiracy, he caused her to be thrown out of the Window, and her Blood was sprinkled on the Wall, and the Dogs afterwards eat her Body, all but her Skull and the Palms of her Hands, pursuant to the Threatnings of the Prophet, as a Punishment for her wickedness, and the Murder of *Naboth*. After which *Jehu* slew 70 of the Sons of *Ahab*, and all his Relations and Friends, and destroy'd all the Priests of *Baal*, having by a Stratagem assembled them all together; and by these Acts of Justice had the Kingdom assur'd to his Posterity of the 4th Generation.

Naaman's leprosie cured II King.[s] 14:

Iezebel's death II:Kings 9:33.

5.14 Then he went down and dipped him:selfe seven times in Iordan &c
9:33 And he said throw her down, so they threw her down and &

The Angels salutation Luc: 1:26

The visitation Luc: 1. 39.

Luc 1:26 And in y̆ sixth month y̆ angell
Gabriel was sent from God unto a &c
Luc: 1:39 And Mary arose in those
dayes and went into y̆ hill countrey

LXXXI. *The* SALUTATION.

THE Time being at Hand, when God, to complete the Predictions of the Prophets, and in Companion to the Sons of Men, was pleased to cause his beloved Son to become incarnate, in order to dispense a new Gospel of Salvation to lost Mankind; the Angel Gabriel was sent to a Virgin, espoused to a Man whose Name was *Joseph*, of the House of *David*, named MARY, to whom he said, *Hail thou that art highly favoured, the Lord is with thee : Blessed art thou amongst Women*. The Virgin being surpriz'd at this Salutation, the Angel bid her fear not ; alluring her, that she, tho a Virgin, should conceive and bring forth a Son, named JESUS, who should be called *the Son of the Highest, who should reign over the House of* Jacob *and whose Kingdom should have no End* : Adding, *That the Holy Ghost should come upon her, and the Power of the Highest should over-shadow her, and the Holy Child to be born, should be called the Son of God. And Mary* said, *Behold the Handmaid of the Lord, Be it unto me according to thy Word*.

LXXXII. *The* VISITATION.

NOW *Elizabeth*, the Wife of *Zacharias*, and Cousin of *Mary*, being miraculously with Child of *John the Baptist* in her old Age, and the Angel *Gabriel* acquainting Mary therewith, as a Proof of his Divine Mission, the Blessed Virgin went to pay a Visit to her Kinswoman ; and as soon as *Elizabeth* heard her Voice, the Babe leaped in her Womb, and she was filled with the Holy Ghost, and said with a loud Voice, *Blessed art thou among Women ! And Blessed is the Fruit of thy Womb : And whence is this to me, that the Mother of my Lord should come to me !* &c.

LXXXIII.

The Angel Appeareth to the Shepherds.

AUGUSTUS *Cæsar* having commanded a general Taxation of all the World, Joseph and his espoused Wife Mary went up to Bethlehem to be taxed; and it happening that the Time of her Delivery arriving, she brought forth her first-born Son, and laid him in a Manger, there being no Room in the Inn. But tho no earthly Pomps attended the Birth of the Prince of Peace, and he was thus obscurely brought into the World, yet the Angel of God proclaimed the joyful Tidings to Men, and appeared to some Shepherds that were keeping their Flocks by Night, surrounded with the Glory of the Lord; and bid the Shepherds fear not; for in that Day a Saviour was born in the City of *David*, whom for a Sign, they should find wrapped in Swaddling Cloaths, lying in a Manger: And suddenly there was with the Angel, a Multitude of the Heavenly Host, praising God, and saying, *Glory be to God in the Highest, and on Earth Peace, Good Will towards Men.*

LXXXIV.

The CIRCUMCISION.

THE Shepherds going to *Bethlehem*, and finding the Child laid in a Manger, as the Angel had said, they divulged every where, to the Admiration of all that heard them, what they had seen and observ'd, and return'd glorifying and praising God. And when eight Days were accomplished for the Circumcising of the Child (according to the Law of *Moses*) his Name was called JESUS, which was so named of the Angel before he was conceived in the Womb.

The angel and ỵ Shepherds. Lu: 2. 10

The Circumcision Luc: 2: 21

Luc: 2:10. And ỵ angell said unto them fear not: for behold I bring ỵ
Luc: 2: 21 And when eight dayes were accomplished for the

Christ preacheth in a ship. Mat: 13:2

The Canaan woman Math: 15:22

Mat: 13:2. And a great multitud gathard together unto him so that he went &c:
Math 15:22: And behold a woman of Canaan came out of the same coasts &c

LXXXV. *CHRIST preacheth in a Ship.*

THE Blessed Jesus, after this increasing in Wisdom and Stature, preached the Kingdom of God to the *Jews*, and went about healing the Sick, curing the Lame, restoring the Blind to Sight, and performing many Miracles ; insomuch, that the Fame of him spread throughout all the neighbouring Nations ; and on a Time sitting by the Sea-side, and seeing great Multitudes about him, he went into a Ship, and as they stood on the Shore, he spake many Things unto them in Parables particularly the Parable of the Sower, who sowed some Seed by the Way-side, which the Fowls of the Air devoured ; some in stony Places, which perish'd after it was sprung up, for want of sufficient Depth ; some among Thorns, which choak'd it ; and some upon good Ground, which produced an hundred-fold ; alluding to the Word of God, sown in the Minds of different Persons of bad and good Inclinations.

LXXXVI. *The Woman of* CANAAN.

THE following History is a pregnant Instance of the Efficaciousness of a lively Faith, and an Encouragement to the contrite Heart to be instant and importunate in Supplications to the Almighty. —— Jesus passing into the Heathen Coasts, *Behold a Woman of* Canaan *cryed unto him, saying, Have Mercy on me, O Lord, thou Son of* David ; *my Daughter is grievously vexed with a Devil. But he answered her not a Word. And his Disciples came and besought him to send her away : But he said, I am not sent but unto the lost Sheep of the House of* Israel. *Then came she, and worshipped him, saying, Lord, help me ! But he answered, It is not meet to take the Childrens Bread, and cast it to Dogs. And she said, Truth, Lord : Yet the Dogs eat of the Crumbs which fall from their Master's Table. Then Jesus said unto her, O Woman, great is thy Faith ! Be it unto thee even as thou wilt. And her Daughter was made whole from that very Hour.*

LXXXVII.

The Buyers and Sellers whipt out of the Temple.

Our Blessed Saviour having ridden triumphantly into *Jerusalem*, with the Acclamations of the Multitude, *He went into the Temple of God, and cast out all them that sold and bought in the Temple, and overthrew the tables of the Money-changers, and the Seats of them that sold Doves; and said unto them, it is written, My House shall be called the House of Prayer, but ye have made it a Den of thieves. And the Lame and the Blind came unto him in the Temple, and he healed them. And when the Chief Priests and Scribes saw the wonderful things that he did, and the Children crying in the Temple, and saying* Hosannah *to the Son of* David*, they were sore displeased, and said unto him, Hearest thou what these say? And Jesus said unto them, Yea; have ye not read, Out of the Mouth of Babes and Sucklings thou hast perfected Praise.*

LXXXVIII.

The Last JUDGMENT.

CHRIST having commanded his Disciples to watch, because they knew not when the Son of Man should come, proceeded to give a Description of the last Great Day: When the Son of Man, says he, *shall come in his Glory, and all the Holy Angels with hurt, then shall he sit upon the throne of his Glory. And before him shall be gather'd all Nations; and he shall seperate them one from another, as a Shepherd divideth his Sheep from the Goats: And he shall set the Sheep on his Right Hand, but the Goats on the Left. Then shall the King say unto them on his Right Hand, Come, ye blessed of my Father, inherit the Kingdom prepared for you from the Foundation of the World,* &c. *Then shall he say also unto them on the Left Hand, Depart from me, ye Cursed, into everlasting Fire, prepared for the Devil and his Angels,* &c.

The buyers & sellers whipt out. Mat: 21.12

The last Iudgment Mat 25. 13

Mat: 21.12 And Iesus went into the
Temple of God and cast out all them &c
Mat: 25. 13 Watch therefore for yee know
neither ỹ day nor ỹ hour wherein &c

The palsy cured Mar: 2:4

Iesus transfigured Mar. 9:2.

Mar: 2:4 And when they saw they
cold not come nigh unto him &c:
Mar 9: 2: And after six dayes Iesus taketh
wth him Peter Iames and Iohn, and &c:

LXXXIX.
CHRIST healeth one Sick of the Palsy.

OUR Saviour having enter'd into *Capernaum*, preached the Word to a prodigious Multitude that was assembled to hear him; and they brought to him a Man sick of the Palsy to be cured; but not being able to come nigh him for the Crowd, they uncover'd the Roof where he was, and let down the Bed, with the Palsy Man upon it; Jesus seeing their Faith, told the sick Man, His Sins were forgiven him: This disgusting the Scribes, who said, No-one could forgive Sins but God, and that he blasphem'd; Jesus ask'd whether was easier, to say to the Sick, *Thy Sins be forgiven thee:* Or to say, *Arise, and take up thy Bed and Walk?* He then as a Proof of his Power to forgive Sins, said to the sick Man, *Arise, and take up thy Bed, and go thy Way into thine House. And immediately he arose, took up the Bed, and went forth before them all, insomuch that they were all amazed, and glorified God, saying, We never saw it on this Fashion!*

XC.
The TRANSFIGURATION.

AND Jesus took with him *Peter*, and *James*, and *John*, and led them up into an high Mountain apart by themselves; and he was transfigured before them. *And his Raiment became Shining, exceeding white as Snow, so as no Fuller on Earth can white them. And there appeared unto them* Elias *with* Moses; *and they were talking with* Jesus. *And there was a Cloud that overshadowed them; and a Voice came out of the Cloud, saying, this is my beloved Son! Hear him.* The three Disciples were extremely surprized at this glorious Sight, and after having recover'd themselves, they looked about, and saw no Man there but their Master; who descending the Mount with them, charged them not to mention what they had seen to any one, till after he was risen from the Dead.

XCI.

CHRIST's *Head anointed.*

NOW when Jesus *was in* Bethany, *in the Houſe of* Simon *the Leper, there came unto him a Woman having an Alabaſter-Box of very precious Ointment, and poured it on his Head, as he ſat at Meat. But when his Diſciples ſaw it, they had Indignation, ſaying, To what Purpoſe is this Waſte ? For this Ointment might have been fold for much, and given to the Poor.* Jeſus *ſaid unto them, Why trouble ye the Woman ? For ſhe hath wrought a good Work upon me : For ye have the Poor always with ye but me ye have not always. For in that ſhe hath poured this Ointment on my Body, ſhe did it for my Burial. Verily I ſay unto you, Whereſoever this Goſpel ſhall be preached in the whole World, there ſhall alſo this that this Woman hath done, be told for a Memorial of her.*

XCII.

The RESURRECTION.

JUDAS having betrayed our Saviour with a kiſs, and he having been ſentenced to Death, by *Pilate*, and crucified between Two Thieves, as is more particularly related in our XCIII, XCIV, XCV, and XCIXth Hiſtories, his Body was delivered to *Joſeph* of *Arimathea*, who wrapt it in fine Linnen, and laid him in a Sepulchre, which was hewn out of a Rock, and rolled a Stone againſt the Door of it. Now *Mary Magdalene*, and *Mary* the Mother of *James* and *Salome*, ſeeing where he was laid, took Spices in order to anoint his Body, and while they were ruminating how they ſhould get the Stone remov'd, found it miraculouſly rowl'd away, and they were ſurprized with the Sight of a young Man on the Right Hand, cloathed all in white, who told them, Chriſt was riſen, and bid them tell his Diſciples ſo, and that they ſhould ſee him in *Galilee*, as he himſelf had promiſed before his Crucifixion.

Christ head anointed Mat: 26:7

His resurrection Mar: 16:1.

Mat: 26:7. Ther came unto him a wo=
man having an alablaster box &c:
Mar: 16:1. And when y̓ Sabath day was
oast, Mary Magdalene and Mary &c

Iesus brought before Pilate Luk. 23. 1.

The Iews crown him wth thorns Ioh: 19: 2.

Luk 23. 18 And they cried out all at once
saying away with this man &c:
Ioh 19. 2: And the soldiers platted a crown
of thornes and put it on his head &c:

XCIII. JESUS *brought before* PILATE.

WE shall now give some further Particulars from the other Evangelists of the Sufferings, Death, and Resurrection of our Blessed Lord, besides the former History, which we extracted from St. *Mark's* Gospel. St. *Luke* tells us, That *Jesus* being seized by Order of the Chief Priests, was led to *Pilate*, the Roman Governor of *Judea*, and accused of perverting the Nation, of forbidding the Payment of Tribute to *Cæsar*, and of calling himself a King. But *Pilate* finding no Fault in him, sent him to *Herod*, who return'd him back to *Pilate*; and as they were before at Enmity together, this Piece of Civility, reconciled them to each other. *Pilate* did all he could to save *Jesus*; and it being the Custom to pardon a Malefactor on Occasion of their Great Feast, he proposed to chastise him, and let him go: But the harden'd *Jews* were so clamorous for his Death, that to appease them, *Pilate* was oblig'd to consent to it, and instead of the Blessed Jesus, released *Barabbas*, a Murderer, and a seditious Person, and deliver'd into their merciless Hands, the Lord of Life and Glory.

XCIV. CHRIST *crowned with Thorns.*

ST. *John* acquaints us, That before *Pilate* delivered *Jesus* into the Hands of the *Jews*, he caused him to be scourged, and that the Soldiers in Derision, platted a Crown of Thorns, and put it on his Head, and having put on him a purple Robe, they mocked him, and said, *Hail, King of the Jews*; bowing the Knee to him, and smiting him with their Hands. *Then came Jesus forth, wearing the Crown of Thorns, and the Purple Robe, and* Pilate *saith unto them, Behold the Man.* And the Chief Priests and Officers cry'd out, *Crucify him, crucify him!* *Pilate*, finding he could not prevail to save him, took Water and washed his Hands, saying, *I am innocent of the Blood of this just Person; see ye to it.* The Jews answer'd, *His Blood be on us and on our Children.* And this Curse, in a terrible Manner, has remained upon them to this Day.

XCV. *The* CRUCIFIXION.

CHRIST being thus deliver'd into the Hands of his inveterate Enemies, they carry'd him to a place called *Golgotha*, where they crucified him between two common Malefactors. And *Pilate* caused the following Title to be fixed to the Cross of Jesus, JESUS OF NAZARETH, THE KING OF THE JEWS. And the Soldiers divided his Garments amongst them; but his Coat being without Seam, they cast Lots for it; that the Scripture might be fulfilled, which saith, *They parted my Raiment among them; and for my Vesture they did cast Lots.* Thus was the Lord of Life put to Death by the barbarous *Jews*, his Mother, and her Sister, and *Mary* the Wife of *Cleophas* and *Mary Magdalene*, standing by the Cross, and lamenting a Catastrophe so deplorable to them; but which was to be the Seal of Redemption to lost Sinners, and an Expiation for the Transgressions of Mankind.

XCVI. CHRIST's RESURRECTION.

WHEN Peter and John were informed, that the body of our Lord was not to be found in the Sepulchre in which he was laid, they hasted thither, and saw the Linnen in which it was wrapped, and the Napkin that was about his Head; which made them believe it was taken away; for as yet, they knew not the Scripture, that he must rise from the Dead. And what made them more surpriz'd was, because *Pilate* had order'd a Watch to be set, and a very great Stone to be rolled against the Door, which was also sealed, by way of Precaution, lest, as the *Jews* suggested to him, the Body shou'd be stollen by his Disciples. But an Angel from Heaven removed the Stone, whose Countenance was like Lightning, and his Raiment white as Snow, who acquainted the Women of our Saviour's Resurrection, as has been mentioned in our XCII History.

The HISTORY of the BIBLE   97

The Crucifixion. Ioh: 19 23

95

Chrsits resurrection Iohn 20:1

96

Ioh: 19: 23. Then the soldiers, when they
had crucified Iesus, took his garments:
Ioh: 20.1 The first day of the weeke cometh
Mary Magdalene early when &c

Lazarus raised XI 38 : Iohn

He washeth y^e desciples feet Iohn 13:5

Jesus therefore again groaning in him:
selfe, cometh to y^e graue, It was a &c
After that he powreth water in to a ba:
son and began to wash y^e disciples &c

XCVII. LAZARUS *Raised.*

NOR was it to be wonder'd, that our blessed Saviour should rise from the Dead, whose Almighty Word, tho veiled in Humanity, was able to raise others to Life. A signal Instance of this, he was pleased to give in raising *Lazarus*, the Brother of *Martha* and *Mary*, whom the Scripture says Jesus loved. This Person had been interred four Days, and was supposed to be turning to Corruption, when Christ came to his Grave; but as nothing is too great for Omnipotence, Jesus order'd them to remove the Stone that was laid over the Grave, and after a short Ejaculation to Almighty God, he cry'd with a loud Voice, *Lazarus, come forth !* And immediately he came forth bound Hand and Feet, with Grave-cloathing, and his Face was bound about with a Napkin; and Jesus commanded them to loose him, and let him go; which was accordingly done, and many of the *Jews*, who beheld this Miracle, were converted, and believed in Christ.

XCVIII. JESUS *washes his Disciples Feet.*

WHEN the Time was near come, that our Blessed Lord should leave this World, and return to his Father, He, in order to give a Lesson of Humility to his Disciples, poured Water into a Bason, and washed their Feet, and wiped them with the Towel wherewith he was girded. But *Peter* making Objections to this Favour, Jesus told him. If he did not wash him, he had no Part with him whereupon *Peter* said, *Lord, not my Feet only, but also my Hands and my Head !* Afterwards he proceeded to acquaint them with the Reason of his Condescension, saying, *Ye call me Master, and Lord: And ye say well ; for so I am. If I then your Lord and Master, have washed your Feet, ye ought also to wash one another's Feet. For I have given you an Example, that ye should do as I have done to you,* &c.

XCIX. JESUS *nailed to the Cross.*

IT must needs be very affecting to sinful Man, when he contemplates the Sufferings which the Blessed Jesus underwent, in order to make an Atonement for our Transgressions: It was the most condescending Goodness in the Lord of Life, to leave the Right Hand of the Almighty, and the Regions of Eternal Blessedness, to become Man, and to vouchsafe to take upon himself our Infirmities, in order to effect the great Work of our Redemption; but voluntarily to subject himself to be despised, and reviled, to be betray'd, and seiz'd upon as a Criminal, to be mocked and scourged, spit upon, and insulted, and to be nailed to the ignominious Cross between two common Malefactors; and all this to save from Perdition, those very Miscreants who inflicted these Barbarities upon him; these are such amazing Instances of Goodness, that none but a JESUS could undergo: And ought to inspire us with stedfast Resolutions to adhere inviolably to his Laws, and his Precepts, that so we may be worthy Partakers of the Merits of his Sufferings, and not render his Sacrifice for our Redemption vain.

C. JESUS *appeareth to* Mary Magdalene.

ST. *John* in his Holy Gospel records, That as *Mary Magdalene* looked into the Sepulchre weeping, she saw two Angels in white, who asked her the Reason of her Tears? She told them, It was because they had taken away the Body of her Lord, and she knew not where they had laid him. Then turning herself, she saw Jesus standing, who said unto her, *Woman, why weepest thou? Whom seekest thou?* She supposing him to be the Gardiner, saith, *Sir, If thou have born Him hence, tell me where thou hast laid him, and I will take him away.* Jesus saith unto her, *Mary!* she turned her self, and saith unto her, *Rabboni,* which is to say, *Master.* Jesus saith unto her, *Touch me not, for I am not yet ascended to my Father: But go to my Brethren, and say unto them, I ascend unto my Father, and your Father and to my God and your God.*

The HISTORY of the BIBLE   101

They nail Iesus to y^e cross. Ioh: 19.18

Iesus appeareth to Mary Magdalen Ioh 20:15

Where they crucified him, and two other wth him on either side, one &c.
Iesus saith unto her woman why weepest thou, whom seekest thou. &c

Zacheus y^e Publican Luke 19:2:

of Cesar's tribute Math: 22:15

Lu: 19:2: And behold there was a
man named Zacheus which was &c
Then went the Pharisees and tooke
counsell how they might &c.

CI. ZACCHEUS *the Publican*.

THE Zeal of *Zaccheus* the Publican, ought not be pafs'd over of in Silence, tho we have not inferted it in its proper Place, before the Paffion of our Bleffed Lord. This Man was very rich, and the Chief among the Publicans, and as *Jefus* paffed thro *Jericho*, he not being able, by Reafon of the Crowd, to fee him, being little of Stature, got up into a Sycamore Tree: As Jefus paffed by, he caft up his Eyes, and faid, Zaccheus, *make hafte, and come down ; for to Day I muft abide at thy Houfe.* And he made hafte, and came down, and received him joyfully. And *Zaccheus* faid unto the Lord, *Behold, Lord, the Half of my Goods I give to the Poor ; and if I have taken any Thing from any Man by falfe Accufation, I reftore him fourfold.* And they all murmuring that he confcended to be a Gueft to a Publican or Sinner, *Jefus* faid, *This Day is Salvation to come to this Houfe, forafmuch as he alfo is the Son of* Abraham. *For the Son of Man is come to feek, and to fave that which was loft.*

CII. *Of paying* TRIBUTE *to* CÆSAR.

ONE of the great Accufations of the *Jews* againft our Bleffed Lord, to Induce *Pontius Pilate* the Governor of *Judea*, to put him to Death, was, That he had forbid paying Tribute to *Cæfar* : The very contrary to this was the Truth ; for when the Pharifees had confulted together to entrap him in his Talk, that they might have a Pretence to wreak their Malice on him, they came to him, flattering him, That they knew he taught the Way of God in Truth, and was no Refpecter of Men ; *Tell us, therefore,* faid they, *what thinkeft thou ? Is it lawful to give Tribute to Cæsar, or not ?* But Jefus perceiving their Wickednefs, said, *Why tempt ye me, ye Hypocrites ? Shew me the Tribute Money.* And they brought him a Penny. And he saith unto them, *Whofe is this Image and Superfcription ?* They anfwer'd *Cæfar's* : He faid, *Render therefore unto Cæfar, the Things that are Cæfar's, and unto God the things that are God's.*

CIII. CHRIST *beareth the Cross.*

ST. Luke acquaints us, That after *Pilate* had given *Jesus* to the Will of the *Jews*, as they led him away, they laid hold of one *Simon* a *Cyrenian*, and put the Cross on him, that he might bear it after *Jesus*. And there followed him a great Company of People, and of Women, which also bewailed him, and lamented him. But *Jesus* turning unto them, said, *Daughters of* Jerusalem, *weep not for me, but weep for your selves, and for your Children. For behold the Days are coming in the which they shall say, Blessed are the Barren, and the Wombs that never bore, and the Paps which never gave suck. Then shall they begin to say to the Mountains, Fall on us; and to the Hills, cover us. For if thy do these things in a green tree, what shall be done in the dry?*

CIV. *The* ASCENSION.

OUR Saviour after his Resurrection, having remained on Earth Forty Days, being seen of his Disciples, and speaking to them of the Things pertaining to the Kingdom of God, after this, assembled them on the Mount called *Olivet*, and there assured them, that they should in a few Days receive the Holy Ghost, and be Witnesses to him, both in *Jerusalem*, and in all *Judea*, and in *Samaria*, and unto the uttermost Part of the Earth. And when he had spoken these Things, while they beheld, he was taken up, and a Cloud received him out of their Sight. And while they looked stedfastly towards Heaven, as he went up, behold, two Men stood by them, in white Apparel; who said unto them, *Ye Men of* Galilee, *Why stand ye gazing up into Heaven? This same* Jesus *which is taken up from you into Heaven, shall so come, in like Manner as ye have seen him go into Heaven.* Then return'd they unto *Jerusalem*, from the Mount *Olivet*, to wait there for the Promise of God, according to the Command of their blessed Master.

The HISTORY *of the* BIBLE   105

Christ beareth his cross Luke 23-26

The ascension of Christ Acts 1.9.

And as they led him away they
laid hold upon one Simon &c.
And when he had spoken these things
while they behold he was taken &c

The coming of y̓ holy Ghost Act: 2:1

Ananias and Sapphira Act: 5:1.

And when y̓ day of Pentecost was fully come they were all with one &c:
But a certain man named Ananias with Sapphira his wife &c

CV. *The Coming of the* HOLY GHOST.

THE Apoſtle having choſen by Lot *Matthias* to fill up the vacant Place of *Judas*, who had betrayed his Lord, and went afterwards and hanged himſelf, ſo that he burſt aſunder in the midſt, and all his Bowels guſhed out ; on the Day of Pentecoſt, they aſſembled all together in one Place, and ſuddenly there came a Sound from Heaven, as of a milling mighty Wind, and it filled all the Houſe where they were ſitting. And there appeared unto them eleven Tongues, like as of Fire, and it ſat upon each of them. And they were all filled with the Holy Ghoſt, and began to ſpeak with other Tongues, as the Spirit gave them Utterance. At the Rumor of this Prodigy, a mix'd Multitude of ſeveral Nations aſſembled together, and in the greateſt Amazement, ſaid one to another, *Behold, are not all theſe that ſpeak* Galileans *? And how hear we every Man in our own Tongue wherein we were born !* Parthians *and* Medes, *and* Elamites, *and the Dwellers in* Meſopotamia, *&c.*

CVI. ANANIAS *and* SAPPHIRA.

AFTER the Apoſtles had received the Holy Ghoſt, they performed ſeveral great Miracles in the Name of Jeſus, and Converted many Thouſands to the Faith of Chriſt, who conſtantly followed them ; and lived all in common, and wanted nothing, for thoſe who had Eſtates and Poſſeſſions ſold them, and brought the Money to the Apoſtles, who divided it equally among the Faithful. But a certain Man named *Ananias*, with his Wife *Sapphira*, having ſold their Poſſeſſions, and kept back Part, brought it to the Apoſtles, pretending it was the Whole. This being an Endeavour by a Lye to impoſe on the Holy Ghoſt, *Peter* ſeverely rebuked *Ananias*, ſo that he fell down dead at his Feet; and his Wife coming in afterwards, not hearing what had happen'd, inſiſted in the ſame Story, and alſo fell down dead, as her Husband had done ; and left a terrible Example of the Wickedneſs of a counterfeit Zeal for God's Glory, *&c.*

CVII. PHILIP *baptizeth the* EUNUCH.

PHILIP having converted *Samaria*, and great Multitudes of People to the Faith of Chrift, as he was going from *Jerufalem* to *Gaza*, according to the Direction of an Angel of the Lord, met with an Eunuch of great Authority, and chief Treafurer to *Candace*, Queen of Æthiopia, who was fitting in his Chariot, and reading in *Efaias* the Prophet, thefe Words, *He was Led as a Sheep to the Slaughter, and like a Lamb dumb before his Shearer, fo opened he not his Mouth*, &c. *Philip* asking the Eunuch, If he underftood what he read ? The Eunuch anfwered No, and defired him to come into his Chariot, and explain that Text to him : *Philip* complying with his Requeft, preached to him Jefus fo powerfully, that the Eunuch was converted, and as they rode, being come to a certain Water, he prevailed on *Philip* to alight, and baptize him into the Faith of Chrift, profeffing his Belief, that Jefus was the Son of God. Which being done, *Philip* was caught away by the Spirit of God, and the Eunuch faw him no more, but went on rejoycing.

CVIII. PETER *let out of Prifon by an* ANGEL.

HEROD feeing the great Progrefs made by the Apoftles in Chriftianity, raifed up a Perfecution againft them, and killed *James* the Brother of *John* with the Sword, and caufing *Peter* to be apprehended, he caft him into Prifon, intending after *Eafter* to bring him forth to the *Jews*, who were pleafed with his Cruelties towards the new Chriftians. But the Night before *Herod* intended to bring him forth, an Angel of the Lord bid *Peter* arife, and follow him, and his Chains fell from off his Hands : And tho the Keeper kept Watch without, as two Soldiers did within, and tho he was to pafs two Wards, and an Iron Gate, yet he following the Angel, efcaped undifcovered of them all, the Iron Gate opening of its own Accord at the Angel's Approach.

Philip baptized ỹ Euuch Acts 38:

Peter led out of Prison Act: 12

And hee comanded ỹ Chariot to stand still and they went down &c.
And behold ỹ Angell of ỹ Lord came upon him and a light &c

110   *The* HISTORY *of the* BIBLE

Saul's conversion Act: 9: 4

The Iaylor converted Act 16. 27

And he fell to ye earth and heard
a voyce saying unto him Saul, &c
And ye keeper of ye prison awaking
out of his sleep and seeing the &c:

CIX. SAUL's Conversion.

AMONG all the Persecutors of the first Christians, no one exerted himself so vehemently against them as *Saul*, who was also called *Paul*, and became afterwards the great Apostle of the Gentiles. He, as the Scripture says, breathing out Threatnings and Slaughter against the Disciples of the Lord, obtained Letters from the High-Priest, to the Synagogues of *Damascus*, that he might bring bound to *Jerusalem*, all that he found professing the Religion of Jesus. But as he came wear to *Damascus*, there suddenly shone round about him a Light from Heaven, and he fell to the Earth, and heard a Voice, saying to him, Saul, Saul, *Why persecutest thou me?* And he said, *Who art thou, Lord?* And the Lord said, *I am Jesus whom thou persecutest? It is hard for thee to kick against the Pricks.* Upon this, resigning himself to the Divine Direction, he went to *Damascus*, and after he had remained blind three Days, was restored to Sight by *Ananias*; and from the bloodied Persecutor, became the most zealous Confessor and Apostle.

CX. The JAYLOR Converted.

PAUL after this, in the Name of the Lord, caused a Spirit of Divination to depart from a Damsel possessed with it, whose Masters being used to make Gains by her Means, so inraged at it, that they procured *Paul* and *Silas* to be beaten with many Stripes, and thrown into Prison. At Midnight the Jaylor having been alarmed with a great Noise, and an Earthquake which had burst open the Prison Doors, imagined all his Prisoners had escaped, and was going to make himself away: But Paul calling out to him, assured him, they were all there, and so prevented his Design. Whereupon the Jaylor was converted to the Faith of Christ, and he and all his Family were baptized, and Paul received great Kindness from him, and was soon deliver'd from his Confinement with Honour.

CXI. St. PAUL *Accused before* FELIX.

AFTER many Miracles perform'd by St. *Paul*, and proselyting great Numbers to the Christian Religion, he was at last apprehended at *Jerusalem* by the *Jews*, and would have been put to Death, had it not been for the chief Captain of the *Romans* in that City, who finding the *Jews* implacably bent to destroy him, sent him under a Guard to *Cæsarea*, the Residence of *Felix*, and chief *Roman* Governor of *Judea*, who finding the *Jews* unable to prove any Thing worthy of Death against him, used him with Lenity ; and after certain Days sent for him, his Wife *Drusilla*, a *Jewess*, being present, and heard him concerning the Faith in Christ ; and as he reasoned of Righteousness, Temperance, and Judgment to come, *Felix* trembled, and answer'd, *Go thy Way for this Time* ; *when I have a convenient Season, I will send for thee*. But after two Years, *Portius Festus* came into *Felix* Room, and *Felix*, willing to shew the *Jews* a Pleasure, left *Paul* bound.

CXII. St. PAUL *bit by a Viper*.

THIS great Apostle had at last, no other Way left to escape the Malice of the *Jews*, but by appealing to *Cæsar* himself, and being put in a Ship, in order to be sent to *Rome*, they were overtaken by a violent Storm, in which having run the greatest Hazard, they were cast in Safety on the Island of *Melita*, now called *Malta*. The People of the Island shewed them great Kindness in their Distress, and made them a Fire to warm them ; but when St. *Paul* had gather'd a Bundle of Sticks, and laid them on the Fire, a Viper came out of the Heat, and fasten'd on his Hand, which made the Company conclude him to be an ill Man, and that tho' he had escaped the Shipwreck, Vengeance suffer'd him not to live : But when they saw him shake off the Viper into the Fire, without receiving any Harm, they changed their Minds, and said he was a God. And he continued there three Months curing the Sick, and healing all manner of Diseases.

The HISTORY of the BIBLE 113

Paul accused Act: 24: 24.

111

Paul bit wth a Viper Act: 28: 3.

112

And after certain dayes when Felix
came wth his wife Drusilla &c:
And when Paul had gathered a
bundle of sticks and laid &c:

The starr fall from heaven. 6.13

The tribes sealed Rev: 7 : 1.

6.13. And yͤ starrs of heaven fell unto yͤ earth &c.
7.1. And after these things I saw four angels standing &c

CXIII. *The* S T A R S *fall from Heaven.*

THE bleſſed Evangeliſt St. *John* aſſures us, that God ſignified to him by an Angel, the Things that muſt ſhortly come to paſs, which he therefore calls the *Revelation of Jeſus Chriſt,* and which we ſhall briefly recite in his very Words ; not preſuming to offer at any Expoſition of thoſe Holy Myſteries, which have appeared ſo intricate to the greateſt Divines, that it was the Saying of a learned Man, that he never knew any one offer to expound this myſterious Book, *but it found him mad, or left him ſo.*

After the Evangeliſt had mentioned the Lamb opening five Seals, he proceeds : And when he had opened the ſixth Seal, lo ! there was a great Earthquake, and the Sun became black, and the Moon Blood, and the Stars fell to the Earth, and the Heaven departed as a Scroul rolled together, and every Mountain and Iſland was moved out of their Places ; and the Kings of the Earth, and mighty Men hid themſelves in Dens, and in the Rocks of the Mountains, and ſaid to the Rocks and Mountains, Fall on us, and hide us from the Face of him that ſitteth on the Throne, and from the Wrath of the Lamb ; For the great Day of his Wrath is come, and who ſhall be able to ſtand ?

CXIV. *The* T R I B E S *ſealed.*

AND after theſe Things, I ſaw four Angels, ſtanding on the four Corners of the Earth, holding the four Winds of the Earth, that the Wind ſhould not blow upon the Earth, nor the Sea, nor on any Tree. And I ſaw another Angel aſcending from the *Eaſt,* having the Seal of the living God, and he cried with a loud Voice to the four Angels, Hurt not the Earth, neither the Sea, nor the Trees, till we have ſealed the Servants of our God in their Forehead. And there were ſealed an Hundred and Forty and Four Thouſand of all the Tribes of the Children of *Iſrael.*

CXV.
The Grafs and Trees fired.

AND another Angel came and stood at the Altar, having a golden Censer, and the Angel filled the Censer with Fire of the Altars, and cast it into the Earth, and there were Noises and Thunderings, and Lightnings, and an Earthquake. And the seven Angels which had the seven Trumpets prepared themselves to sound. The first Angel sounded, and there followed Hail and Fire mingled with Blood, and they were cast upon the Earth and the third Part of Trees was burnt up, and all green Grass was burnt up.

CXVI.
The Seven Angels sound.

AND the 2d Angel sounded, and the third Part of the Sea became Blood, and the 3d Part of the Creatures in the Sea died, and the 3d Part of the Ships were destroy'd. And the third Angel sounded, and there fell a great Star from Heaven called *Wormwood* upon the 3d Part of the Rivers and Fountains, and many Men died of the Waters, because they were bitter. And the 4th Angel sounded, and the 3d Part of the Sun, Moon, and Stars were darken'd. And the 5th Angel sounded, and a Star fell from Heaven unto Earth, and to him was given the Key of the Bottomless Pit, out of which arose a Smoke, and out of the Smoke Locusts, which had the Power of Scorpions, to torment for five Months all those Men who had not the Seal in their Foreheads. And the 6th Angel sounded, who had Cords to loose the four Angels which were bound in the great River *Euphrates*, with intent to slay the 3d Part of Men. But in the Days of the Voice of the 7 th Angel, when he shall begin to sound, the Mystery of God shall be finish'd, as he hath declared to his Servants the Prophets.

The corn, grass, or trees, fired 8.7

The seven Angels sounds 8:2

8:7. The first angell sounded
and there followed hail &c.
8:2. And I saw yͤ seven angel͛
which stood before god &c.

Satan's rage Rev: 13:1

Rev: 14 1 The Lamb on Sion

13:1: And I stood upon y͜e Sand of y͜e
and saw a beast rise up out of: &c
14:1: And I looked & loe, a Lambe sto
od on y͜e mount Sion, &c.

CXVII.
Satan's Rage ; Or, The Beaſt with Seven Heads.

ST. *John* then tells us, That he ſtood upon the Sand of the Sea, and ſaw a Beaſt like a Leopard riſe up out of the Sea, having Seven Heads and Ten Horns, and upon his Head the Name of *Blaſphemy :* That his Feet were as the Feet of a Bear, and his Mouth as that of a Lyon, with which he blaſphem'd the Name of God, and his Tabernacle : That Power was given him over all Kindred, Tongues and Nations, and that all thoſe Whoſe Names were not written in the Book of Life, worſhipped him. He declares, That he ſaw another Beaſt coming up out of the Earth as this did out of the Sea, having Two Horns like a Lamb, and he ſpoke as a Dragon, and perform'd great Wonders, making Fire come down from Heaven in the Sight of Men, whom he deceived by his Miracles and cauſed all, both Small and Great, Rich and Poor, Free and Bond, to receive a Mark in their Right Hand, or in their Foreheads, that no Man might Buy or Sell, ſave he that had the Mark or Name of the Beaſt.

CXVIII.
The LAMB *on* SION.

AND lo, a Lamb ſtood on the Mount *Sion*, and with him an Hundred and Forty and Four Thouſand, having his Father's Name written in their Foreheads — And in their Mouth was found no Guile. And I ſaw another Angel fly in the midſt of Heaven, having the everlaſting Goſpel, ſaying with a loud Voice, *Fear God, and give Glory to him, for the Hour of his Judgment is come* — And there followed another Angel, ſaying, Babylon *is fallen, is fallen.* — And the third Angel followed, ſaying with a loud Voice, *If any Man worſhip the Beaſt and his Image, and receive his Mark, the ſame ſhall drink of the Wine of the Wrath of God, and he ſhall be tormented with Fire and Brimſtone.*

CXIX. *The* EARTH *Reaped.*

AND I looked, and behold, , a white Cloud, and upon the Cloud one fat like unto the Son of Man, having on his Head a golden Crown, and in his Hand a sharp Sickle. And an Angel cry'd with a loud Voice to him that fat on the Cloud, *Thruſt in thy Sickle, and reap — for the Harveſt of the Earth is ripe* — And he thruſt in his Sickle, and the Earth was reaped. And another Angel came out of Heaven, having alſo a sharp Sickle ; to whom a third Angel cried, *Thruſt in thy ſharp Sickle, and gather the Cluſters of the Vine of the Earth, for her Grapes are full ripe.* And the Angel did ſo, and gathered the Vine of the Earth, and caſt it into the great Wine-preſs of the Wrath of God. And the Wine-preſs was troden without the City, and Blood came out of the Wine-preſs, *&c*

CXX.

The VIALS *of* WRATH.

SEVEN Angels having received ſeven golden Vials full of the Wrath of God, the firſt poured out his Vial upon the Earth ; the ſecond upon the Sea; the third upon the Rivers and Fountains of Water; the fourth, upon the Sun; the fifth, upon the Seat of the Beaſt ; the ſixth, upon the great River *Euphrates* ; and the ſeventh, upon the Air ; and they were followed with ſeven different and terrible Effects of God's Wrath upon that Part of Mankind which worſhipped the Beaſt, and mighty Earthquakes, and Thunderings, and Lightnings ſucceeded. St. *John* tells us alſo, That he ſaw three unclean Spirits, like Frogs, come out of the Mouth of the Dragon, being Spirits of Devils, working Miracles, which go forth unto the Kings of the Earth, to gather them to the Battle of the great Day of God Almighty.

FINIS.

The History of the Bible 121

The earth reaped, Rev: 14. 14:

119

The vials of wrath Rev: 16: 1

120

14:14: And I looked and behold a white cloud & upon the cloud &c
16:1: And there came one of ye seven angels &c.

www.ingramcontent.com/pod-product-compliance
Lightning Source LLC
Chambersburg PA
CBHW070924160426
43193CB00011B/1571